flavours of Tuscany

recipes from the heart of Italy

flavours of **Tuscany**

recipes from the heart of Italy

Maxine Clark

photography by Peter Cassidy

RYLAND
PETERS
& SMALL

LONDON NEW YORK

First published in the United Kingdom in 2006
by Ryland Peters & Small
20–21 Jockey's Fields
London WC1R 4BW
www.rylandpeters.com

10 9 8 7 6 5 4 3 2 1

Text © Maxine Clark 2006
Design and photographs
© Ryland Peters & Small 2006

ISBN-10: 1 84597 143 4
ISBN-13: 978 1 84597 143 4

A catalogue record for this book
is available from the British Library.

Printed and bound in China.

**Design and photographic
    art direction** Steve Painter
Commissioning Editor
    Elsa Petersen-Schepelern
Editor Rachel Lawrence
Production Manager Patricia Harrington
Art Director Gabriella Le Grazie
Editorial Director Julia Charles
Publishing Director Alison Starling

Food Stylist Maxine Clark
Assistant Food Stylist
    Marcella Libertini
Indexer Hilary Bird

Notes

• All spoon measurements are level, unless otherwise stated.

• Eggs are medium unless otherwise specified. Uncooked or partially cooked eggs should not be served to the very old, frail, young children, pregnant women or those with compromised immune systems.

• Ovens should be preheated to the specified temperature. Recipes in this book were tested using a regular oven. If using a fan-assisted oven, follow the manufacturer's instructions for adjusting temperatures.

Author's Acknowledgements

In loving memory of our dear friend Elsa Petersen-Schepelern (1948–2005) who was part of the Tuscan team and who was responsible for the birth of this book.

Special thanks to my friend and cooking companion, Marcella Libertini. Her local knowledge and infectious enthusiasm proved invaluable both for photography and tracking down antique props and illusive ingredients. She was truly part of our team – 'chi trova un amico, trova un tresoro'.

Special thanks also to Pete and Steve for making everything look so wonderful!

contents

the flavours of Tuscany

Toscana (Tuscany) derives its name from its 11th century BC founders, the mysterious and cultured Etruscans, and was renamed *Tuscia* when dominated by the Roman Empire in the 3rd century BC. It has had a glorious past, especially during the Renaissance when Italy was dominated by city-states. The capital of Tuscany, Florence was one of the wealthiest and most influential city-states in the land, both in trade and artistic achievement. The terrain, climate and geography of the area means that Tuscany is abundant with produce from the land but, despite its rich legacy, Tuscan cuisine has remained simple and rustic.

Tuscans love bold natural flavours unadorned by sauces and copious amounts of cream and butter. Bread and salt play an important part in this hearty cuisine, day-old bread is used for bruschetta or added to soups to make them more hearty. Although Tuscan bread is famous for being salt-free, the rest of the cuisine certainly isn't. Cooks and chefs here tend to be heavy-handed with the salt. Braising with wine, sage, rosemary, black pepper and salt enhances the flavour of the natural ingredients.

Meats and poultry are plainly grilled on an open wood fire, and spatchcocking (splitting a bird open and flattening it, so that it cooks evenly) is a popular technique. The countryside is diverse with woods, hills, plains and a long coastline so game (wild boar, venison, hare and pheasant) and wild mushrooms are abundant, as is fish (both fresh and salted). You cannot fail to realize when visiting this place that Tuscans have earned the nickname of *mangia fagioli* (bean eaters) and they do love beans both fresh and dried in soups, such as *La Ribollita* (page 31), and in salads and pasta dishes. The cheese of Tuscany is pecorino, which is made from sheep's milk and ranges from soft and fresh to mature for grating and can be bought in every shape, size and colour.

I believe one of the best places to be in the world for those who love really good food and truly remarkable wines is Tuscany. My favourite times to visit are spring and autumn. In spring, the blossom dusts the hedgerows like confetti and the lush countryside is a dazzling tapestry of vibrant and dazzling greens, signalling the arrival of long-awaited tender new vegetables and salads. The weather can be gloriously sunny, even balmy, changing suddenly to driving rain and gusty winds, which is perfect for the new growing season. This is the time for the serious foodie to sample everything green – tender young broad beans, locally picked salad greens foraged straight from the roadside, and pile upon pile of artichokes in every green and violet hue.

In autumn, the damp, thick air is charged with the earthy scents so particular to the region. The leaves on the vines and on the sweet chestnut trees are turning to shades of yellow ochre, raw sienna, burnt sienna, raw umber, scarlet and crimson lake. They flutter down from the trees, then lie in deep musty carpets often hiding edible treasures in their folds. This is a season of mists – they shroud the rolling, wooded, juniper-clad hills, tranquil valleys and expectant vineyards in the early morning, only to vanish as the sun warms away the night's chill. The weather is changeable – lots of rain followed by warm sunshine and cool evenings. Just the sort of conditions to promote the growth of porcini mushrooms and white truffles. These Tuscan treasures lurk beneath the soil, their repose interrupted by a snuffling truffle pig or dog intoxicated by their pungent scent. They are delicately dug out of the soil, carefully pocketed and sold to local restaurants or exported abroad, destined for upmarket delicatessens. Spend a holiday here, and you can eat risotto or pasta swathed in shaved or grated white truffle at a fraction of the price back home. White truffle eating is a unique pleasure, almost primeval in its all-pervading earthiness. It goes with anything that will accommodate its strong flavour, such as eggs, pasta or plain risotto.

Local bakers make *Schiacciata con Uva* (page 145) only in autumn – enormous trays of flat bread studded with Sangiovese grapes, which burst during cooking and stain the dough with wine-coloured juices. It is a real taste of the *vendemmia* (grape harvest) and the new wine to come.

Olives for oil and vines for wine were once grown together, and this method of planting can occasionally be seen today. Although production is relatively small, Tuscan olive oils are some of the best in Italy and have a slightly peppery after-taste. Tuscan wines are big, red and generous, based on the native Sangiovese grape. They owe their existence to the varied terrain and temperate climate of the Tuscan hills, each wine taking on the character of its particular *terroir*. The wines of Tuscany complement the intense rich food, whether it be a simple young Chianti or an aged Brunello di Montalcino, there is one to suit every dish. Never miss an opportunity to sample a glass of Vin Santo, the local dessert wine – every wine producer makes his own and no two are ever the same. Meals are ended simply with fruit in season, picked at optimum ripeness, or with Cantuccini biscuits to dip in Vin Santo. There are few desserts here, but local specialities such as *Ricciarelli* (page 137) and the exotic fruit and spice concoction *Panpepato* (page 142) are eaten on special occasions.

Each of the ten provinces of Tuscany (Massa Carrara, Lucca, Pistoia, Prato, Firenze, Arezzo, Livorno, Pisa, Siena and Grossetto) has something different to offer in the way of local food specialities and wines, making this a truly fascinating area to visit and keep visiting. There is always something new to see and taste, a *sagra* or *festa* to take part in, or a new restaurant to discover and I hope that these recipes will bring some of these delights into your home.

antipasti
starters and nibbles

OLIO EXTRA
VERGINE di OLIVA

olives and olive oil

Revered by the Romans and the Greeks, the olive is one of the oldest and most powerful of all Mediterranean symbols. The olive symbolizes holiness in Christianity and the olive branch is an international symbol of peace. Olive oil is full of health-giving properties – its low-cholesterol content is beneficial for the heart and its high percentage of vitamin E makes it a great skin cream.

Tuscany produces some of Italy's most highly prized olive oils – fragrant, green and rich in flavour and colour. Olive trees prosper on chalky, stony ground with good exposure to the sun, and careful tree management and production methods are vital for good-quality olive oil. Every sub-region of Tuscany has its own, distinctive oil, depending on the geographical position, the method of production and the blend of olive varieties. Some of the best oils are from the Maremma hills, near Livorno, due to their proximity to the sea, the high position of the olive groves and the steady temperate climate which allows the olives to mature slowly. The other principle olive-producing areas are the Florentine hills, the Chianti hills and the Siena area, which produce assertive and slightly bitter oils as well as the area around Lucca, which produces a lighter and sweeter oil.

There are various associations committed to the production of good-quality olive oil. The *Associazione Italiana Agricoltori Biologici* (Italian Association of Organic Farmers) concentrates on the best methods of cultivation and the maintenance of the trees, as well as the production of oil. The *Consorzio Olivicoltori della Toscana Centrale* (Union of Olive Growers of Tuscany) guarantees a consistency of quality and flavour and a very low acidity, and produces some of the best extra virgin olive oil in central Tuscany.

Depending on the weather and the ripening rate of the olives, the olive harvest starts between late October and mid-December. Unripe green olives are picked first for preserving in brine, as they are unsuitable for oil. The main crop is left until it is slightly underripe and a dark purple colour, and these make the best oil. Black and shiny, fully ripe olives are used to balance the flavour of the oil and are harvested in various ways. The traditional way was to spread nets under the trees and wait for the olives to drop off the branches, or hit the trunk with a large wooden stick to speed up their descent. There are now machines that vibrate the trees, shaking the olives off onto nets, although this can damage the large root system of the tree. The best olives for oil are hand-picked just before they are ripe, which is labour-intensive, but saves damage to the precious trees.

Clockwise from top left: pruning and sweeping olive tree branches in spring; olive tree; cured green olives; extra virgin olive oil sign; olive oil from the first pressing; local extra virgin olive oil; cured black olives.

The olives are then taken to an olive mill to be pressed. Artisan olive mills still use traditional millstones, but modern stainless steel continuous presses are easier to control and can produce stunning results. In the first, 'cold', pressing, the olives are washed and ground to a pulp, which is then heated to 15°C (59°F) to release the oil. The pulp is then kneaded to release the oil further, spread onto round mats stacked up around a pole and more oil is squeezed out using a hydraulic press. The oil is spun to remove excess water and may be filtered. The hard cake of residue, known as *sansa*, is sold to large factories to extract more oil by chemical means, giving a highly refined and flavourless pale yellow oil.

Extra virgin olive oil (*olio extravergine d'oliva*) must have an acidity of less than 1%. The acidity level depends on the quality of the olives, their maintenance and the method of pressing. It is the best olive oil to use for drizzling on salads, soups, bruschetta and vegetables, and anointing grilled and roasted meat. *Olio sopraffino vergine d'oliva* (less than 1.5% acidity), *olio fino vergine d'oliva* (less than 3% acidity) and *olio vergine d'oliva* (less than 4% acidity) are more economical and are used for frying. *Olio nuovo* is oil pressed from green, underripe olives and has quite a powerful flavour, while *olio santo* is flavoured with chilli pepper.

The very best olive oil should be used within a year of bottling, otherwise it will lose its texture, flavour and colour. Store it in a cool place, rather than next to the cooker. Wine-style boxes are a good way to purchase olive oil as no air can get in and the oil is kept in the dark. Price is usually a good indicator of quality, as good oil does not come cheap. Single estate extra virgin olive oils are more expensive than blends of good Italian extra virgin olive oils. Supermarket own-brand extra virgin olive oils can be a blend of oils from more than one country, thus keeping the price down, but are perfectly good for everyday cooking. It's a myth that you can't deep-fry in extra virgin olive oil – you can, and the food tastes sublime, but attempt this only if you own an olive grove!

Whole olives are cured in brine to preserve them. Unripe, green olives are inedible and must first be soaked in water or brine to extract the bitterness. Mid-ripe, light-purple olives usually turn greyish green or pink when cured. Fully ripe black olives tend to change to deep purple. The olives are washed, slit to the stone, then placed in a tall jar and covered with brine. They are weighed down to keep them submerged, kept in a cool place for a week and stirred occasionally. Every week for 3–6 weeks, they are rinsed and the brine is changed, which removes the bitterness. A white foam forms on the surface of the brine, but it is harmless as long as the olives do not come into contact with the air. Once cured, the olives can be rinsed, dried and marinated in oil or vinegar with all sorts of herbs and spices.

fettunta al fomaggio

The word *fettunta* is Tuscan dialect for 'anointed slice' – literally, a grilled piece of bread rubbed with garlic and anointed with oil. It must be made with really good sourdough bread, the best and fruitiest olive oil and young, almost nutty, pecorino.

4 large thick slices country bread, preferably sourdough bread
1–2 garlic cloves, halved
extra virgin olive oil, for drizzling and to serve
180 g young pecorino, thinly sliced or roughly grated
6 fresh sage leaves
2 ripe pears, halved, cored and thinly sliced
freshly ground black pepper
watercress, to serve (optional)

serves 6

Barbecue, toast or griddle the bread on both sides and rub one side with garlic and drizzle with olive oil, then put on a baking sheet. Cover the bread with thinly sliced pecorino, then lay a sage leaf on top of each one followed by a fan of three slices of pear. Season with plenty of black pepper and drizzle with oil. Cook in a preheated oven at 200°C (400°F) Gas 6 for about 5 minutes until the cheese is just melted. Serve immediately on a bed of watercress, if liked, with extra olive oil on the table.

chicken liver crostini
crostini di fegatini

Endless variations of these crostini are served all over Tuscany – some good, most bad – but made well, they are utterly delicious. Chicken livers are firm and plump in Italy, so try to buy fresh not frozen, flabby ones. It is traditional to make the topping into a smooth pâté, but I prefer a rougher texture. I add Vin Santo (page 154) to give a rich depth of flavour and a slight sweetness to the chicken livers.

1 Italian sfilatino or small thin French baguette
3 tablespoons extra virgin olive oil, plus extra for brushing
85 g butter
2 shallots, finely chopped
1 celery stick, finely chopped
1 small carrot, finely chopped
175 g fresh chicken livers, trimmed and roughly chopped
2 tablespoons Vin Santo or dry sherry
1 tablespoon sun-dried tomato paste or tomato purée
2 tablespoons salted capers, rinsed and chopped
3 tablespoons chopped fresh parsley, plus extra to garnish
sea salt and freshly ground black pepper

serves 4

Slice the bread into thin rounds, brush both sides with olive oil and spread out on a baking sheet. Bake in a preheated oven at 190°C (375°F) Gas 5 for about 10 minutes until golden and crisp. Keep warm.

Heat the 3 tablespoons of olive oil and half the butter in a frying pan and gently fry the shallot, celery and carrot until softened. Stir in the chicken livers, increase the heat and cook until browned. Add the Vin Santo and tomato paste and simmer for 15 minutes until the liquid has all but evaporated.

Mix in the remaining butter, capers, parsley, and salt and pepper. Pile onto the crostini, sprinkle with parsley and serve immediately.

crostini of dark green cabbage
crostini di cavolo nero

Cavolo nero is a type of dark green cabbage with long separate leaves. It resembles a mini palm tree when growing, and is at its best harvested after being slightly frosted. The nearest equivalent in taste and texture would be savoy cabbage or even kale, but the flavour is unique and really comes alive when sautéd with peppery Tuscan olive oil and garlic.

1 Italian sfilatino or small thin French baguette
3 tablespoons extra virgin olive oil, plus extra for brushing
300 g cavolo nero or savoy cabbage
2–3 garlic cloves, thinly sliced
1 tablespoon balsamic vinegar
sea salt and freshly ground black pepper
fresh herbs, to garnish

serves 6

Slice the bread into thin rounds, brush both sides with olive oil and spread out on a baking sheet. Bake in a preheated oven at 190°C (375°F) Gas 5 for about 10 minutes until golden and crisp. Keep warm.

Divide the cabbage into leaves and cut out the tough stalks. Shred the cabbage as finely as you can. Heat the 3 tablespoons of olive oil in a frying pan, add the garlic and sauté for 1 minute until just turning golden. Add the cabbage, a splash of water, salt and pepper and stir-fry until it completely wilts. Sprinkle the vinegar over the cabbage and stir-fry for another minute until the vinegar disappears. Pile onto the warm crostini, drizzle with more oil and grind over more black pepper. Serve immediately, garnished with fresh herbs.

deep-fried sage leaves
salvia fritta

24 large sage leaves, with stalks
1 teaspoon capers, rinsed and chopped
1 tablespoon anchovy paste
200 ml light beer, chilled
110 g plain white flour
vegetable oil, for deep-frying
sea salt

a deep-fryer

makes 12

Once tasted, never forgotten! I ate these at a friend's wedding reception one hot July day – mounds of them just kept appearing and, needless to say, they went down a treat with the Prosecco. They can be simply dipped in batter and fried or can be sandwiched together with a savoury paste of anchovy and caper. The sandwiches can be prepared well in advance, ready to be fried at the last minute. I sometimes use an instant Japanese tempura batter for convenience as it keeps nice and crisp.

Wash and dry the sage leaves thoroughly. Mix the capers with the anchovy paste and spread onto the darker green side of the leaves. Press another leaf firmly on top to form a sandwich.

Season the flour with salt, then whisk in the beer until the mixture is smooth and has the consistency of double cream.

Heat the oil in a deep-fryer or wok to 180°C (350°F) – a piece of stale bread dropped in should turn golden in a few seconds. Holding the leaves by the stem, dip into the batter and lightly shake off the excess. Drop into the hot oil a few at a time and fry until crisp and barely golden. This will only take a few seconds. Drain on kitchen paper and serve straight away sprinkled with a little salt.

anchovies marinated in lemon and chilli
acciughe o alici al limone e peperoncino

There's nothing quite like a dish of these light tasting, fresh, silvery morsels eaten fillet by fillet with a chilled glass of *vino bianco*. If you've never tried a fresh anchovy before and see some in a market, buy them! They have a mild flavour, not at all like the canned fillets in oil. Fresh anchovies like these are even found on the glorious fish counters of larger supermarkets in Italy. You can, however, substitute very small sardines or even sprats.

Wash the anchovies. Cut off the heads and slit open the bellies. Remove the guts (they aren't substantial) under running water. Slide your thumb along the backbone to release the flesh along its length. Take hold of the backbone at the head end and lift it out. The fish should now be open up like a book. At this stage you can decide whether to cut into two long fillets or leave whole – size will dictate. Pat them dry with kitchen paper.

Put the lemon juice in a shallow non-reactive dish, add the chilli and lay the anchovies in an even layer, skin side up. Cover and marinate in the refrigerator for 24 hours.

The next day, lift them out of the juice (they will look pale and 'cooked') and lay them on a serving dish. Strew them with the spring onions and parsley and liberally anoint with olive oil. Season with salt and pepper and serve at room temperature.

16 fresh anchovies, small sardines or sprats
freshly squeezed juice of 2 lemons
1 small dried red chilli, deseeded and finely chopped
2 large spring onions, thinly sliced
2 tablespoons chopped fresh parsley
extra virgin olive oil, for drizzling
sea salt and freshly ground black pepper

serves 4

Whilst shooting the photographs for this book, our friend Marcella took us to an artichoke festival in Chiusure, a lovely little hilltop village between Siena and Montepulciano. It was the last weekend in April, and a beautiful blue-skied, sun-kissed day. The village was alive with animated people wandering through the narrow streets, passing stalls selling local products. But the central focus of the *festa* was The Artichoke of Chiusure. This small purply-green artichoke has been grown in the area since time immemorial (it is said that the Etruscans bred it from the indigenous wild cardoon) and the locals are fiercely proud of it. A collective of local farmers are saving it from extinction by cultivating it in their market gardens. Its particular flavour comes from the land where it is cultivated, the *crete*, which has a high lime and clay content.

Everywhere you looked at the festival there were boxes, vans and motorcycles laden with these leafy edible thistles. Our photographer, Pete, dashed off to explore the maze of little streets and passageways and found a small striped pavilion perched on the ramparts, where a group of farmers were preparing artichokes for frying. We were offered glasses of wine in plastic cups from their black artichoke-stained hands, and piping hot-fried artichokes in paper napkins. There was much discussion about why we were there and why they were so proud of their artichokes. What a day it was, and there are *festas* and *sagras* like this all over Italy whenever particular produce is in season.

pan-fried artichokes
carciofi fritti

3 large ripe lemons

8–12 medium purply-green artichokes with stems, heads about 10 cm long

8 tablespoons olive oil

2 garlic cloves, sliced

1 tablespoon chopped fresh nepitella or oregano

1 tablespoon tomato purée dissolved in 150 ml vegetable stock or water

sea salt and freshly ground black pepper

serves 4

This is the way artichokes are cooked and eaten in the countryside in Tuscany, the tomato sauce reducing and turning a mahogany colour. An even simpler way to cook artichokes is to prepare them as below, then dip the quarters in seasoned flour and shallow-fry in ordinary olive oil for 3–4 minutes until golden and tender. Drain them on kitchen paper, sprinkle with salt and eat them piping hot.

First prepare the artichokes. Fill a big bowl with water, halve the lemons and squeeze in the juice of 4 halves to acidulate it. Use the remaining lemon halves to rub the cut portions of each artichoke as you work. Starting at the base, snap off the tough purply-green outer leaves, then trim the stalk down to about 5 cm. Trim away the dark green outer layer at the base and peel the fibrous outside of the stalk. Cut about 1 cm off the tip of each artichoke, then place in the lemony water until needed, to prevent discoloration.

Drain the artichokes and pat dry with kitchen paper. Cut each artichoke into quarters and remove any fine hairs (the choke) with a teaspoon. Heat the oil in a large frying pan and sauté the artichokes with the garlic and herbs for 5 minutes until golden. Add the diluted tomato purée, season with salt and pepper, then simmer, uncovered, for 10 minutes. Serve immediately.

marinated baby artichokes
carciofi sott'olio

Tuscans love simple food and this is one of the best ways to prepare fresh artichokes. It is worth donning a pair of light rubber gloves while you prepare them to prevent stained fingers. These young artichokes are quite different from the fat round globe ones. They are slightly smaller than the size of your hand, elongated, purply green in colour and usually sold in bunches. They have very immature chokes inside and I never bother removing them. These are delicious served with fresh *ricotta di pecora*.

3 large lemons
8–12 medium purply-green artichokes with stems, heads about 10 cm long
100 ml extra virgin olive oil, plus extra to serve
100 ml dry white wine
4 sprigs fresh thyme
4 bay leaves
6 whole peppercorns
sea salt

serves 4

First prepare the artichokes. Fill a big bowl with water and squeeze in the juice of ½ lemon to acidulate it. Use the other half of the lemon to rub the cut portions of each artichoke as you work. Starting at the base, snap off the purply-green outer leaves, then trim the stalk down to about 5 cm. Trim away the dark green outer layer at the base and peel the fibrous outside of the stalk. Cut about 1 cm off the tip of the artichoke, then put in the lemony water until needed, to prevent discoloration.

Bring a large pan of salted water to the boil. Drain the artichokes and add to the boiling water. Cook until tender – a sharp knife should pierce easily right to the centre. Drain thoroughly and pile into clean glass jars.

Squeeze the juice from the remaining 2 lemons into a medium saucepan. Add 450 ml water, the olive oil, wine, herbs and peppercorns. Bring to the boil, then simmer for 15 minutes. Pour over the artichokes, covering completely and pushing in the herbs and peppercorns. Cover, cool, then refrigerate for up to 1 week. Serve as an antipasto, with a drizzle of finest olive oil.

spiced baby onions
cipollotti sott'aceto

These wonderful little onions are always included in an *antipasto misto*. They go perfectly with cured meats and salamis. For added depth of flavour, I use a mixture of balsamic vinegar and red wine vinegar, making the liquid a deep red colour. Adding some crushed juniper berries will give them a fragrance from the hills. Use little pickling onions or shallots – red ones are pretty, if you can find them. (See picture, page 8.)

500 g small pickling onions
3 tablespoons balsamic vinegar
about 400 ml red wine vinegar
200 ml red wine
3–4 fresh bay leaves
3 whole cloves or 3 allspice berries, crushed
4 juniper berries, crushed
6 whole peppercorns
sea salt

serves 4

Plunge the onions into boiling water for 2 minutes, then drain well and refresh under cold water. Peel off the skins and trim off the root end, then put them in a large sterilized glass preserving jar.

Put the vinegars, wine, bay leaves, cloves, juniper berries and peppercorns into a medium saucepan and bring to the boil. Boil for 4 minutes, then season with salt and pour over the onions, making sure they are covered. Seal and cool, then keep for about 10 days before using.

pancetta and fennel puffs
còccoli

about 200 ml milk, warmed

50 g lard

40 g fresh yeast or 1 sachet fast-action dried yeast

400 g plain white flour

50 g pancetta, finely diced

1 teaspoon fennel seeds, chopped

vegetable or olive oil, for deep-frying

sea salt

a deep-fryer

serves 8

These 'little darlings' are a type of savoury doughnut or *bomboloni* flavoured with pancetta. I add lightly crushed fennel seeds – a flavouring that is very popular in Tuscany, especially with cured pork. They are deep-fried until crisp on the outside and soft inside and can be kept warm in the oven. Make sure they are piping hot and sprinkled liberally with sea salt when you serve. Grind salt and fennel seeds over them for a special finishing touch. These are especially wonderful if you have the chance to fry them in pure olive oil. The dough can also be rolled out thinly and cut into squares then fried.

Warm the milk with the lard. When melted, crumble in the fresh yeast, if using, and whisk until dissolved. Sift the flour with a good pinch of salt into a bowl and make a well in the centre. If using easy-blend dried yeast, stir it into the flour now. Pour in the warm milk and lard mixture, then add the pancetta and fennel seeds. Mix to a soft dough, adding more flour, if necessary. Form into a ball, cover and leave to rise for 2 hours or until doubled.

Heat the oil in the deep-fryer to 180°C (350°F) – a piece of stale bread dropped in should turn golden in a few seconds. Punch down the dough and knead for 1 minute. Pull off small walnut-sized pieces of dough, about 2 cm, and roll into rough balls. Fry in batches for about 2–3 minutes until pale brown and puffy. Drain well and tip onto kitchen paper. Sprinkle with salt and serve whilst still hot.

fresh broad beans with pecorino and prosciutto
baccelli con pecorino e prosciutto

One of the simplest appetizers in Tuscany is a pile of freshly podded young broad beans served with young pecorino and locally cured *prosciutto crudo*. As simple as that. These springtime beans are called *baccelli*, and are eaten in the Livorno area with a type of lightly salted pecorino-type cheese known as *bacellone*. Another younger, fresh local cheese is *marzolino*, equally delicious. The contrast of fresh green-flavoured beans, creamy, salty cheese and fruity, salty meat is divine. Tuscans eat the beans skins and all, but this is only when the beans are very young.

500 g fresh young unshelled broad beans, or 175 g frozen broad beans, thawed
110 g young pecorino cheese, preferably not the hard grating kind
6 slices Italian dry-cured ham (*prosciutto crudo*)
5 tablespoons olive oil
2 tablespoons freshly squeezed lemon juice
2 teaspoons chopped fresh oregano
2 tablespoons chopped fresh parsley
a pinch of dried chilli flakes (optional)
sea salt and freshly ground pepper

serves 4

Remove the broad beans from their shells, blanch in boiling water for 20 seconds, drain and refresh, then pop them out of their skins and place in a bowl. If using frozen broad beans, thaw then pop them out of their skins and put in a bowl.

Cut the pecorino cheese into cubes and cut the ham into strips, then add to the beans. Whisk together the olive oil, lemon juice, oregano, parsley and pepper flakes, if using, and pour over the bean mixture. Toss together and season to taste with salt and pepper. Serve immediately.

tuscan bread and summer vegetable salad
panzanella

This is one of the most refreshing salads to make and eat on a hot summer's day. My Tuscan friend and occasional help in the kitchen, Antonella, makes the best panzanella – it is light as air and not at all stodgy. Her secret is her light hands. As with pastry, overworking the bread will make it slimy. The bread soaks up the juices from the vegetables and the olive oil and is sharpened by the touch of vinegar. Mix the basil in at the last moment to stop it going black.

2 thick slices stale white country bread (preferably Tuscan saltless bread) at least 1 day old
6 really ripe large tomatoes, deseeded and diced
1 small red onion, finely chopped
½ cucumber, diced
1 small celery stick, diced
1 clove garlic, crushed
6 tablespoons extra virgin olive oil
2 tablespoons red wine vinegar
20 g basil leaves, roughly torn, plus extra to serve
salt and freshly ground black pepper

serves 4

Cut the crusts from the bread and tear into small pieces. Put the bread into a bowl and sprinkle with a couple of tablespoons of cold water. The bread should be only just moist but not soggy. Work the bread with your fingers – like rubbing in butter when making pastry – to distribute the moisture through the bread and break it into smaller crumbs. Lightly mix in two-thirds of the tomatoes, the onion, cucumber, celery and garlic. Drizzle with half the olive oil, add the vinegar, season well with salt and pepper, then toss very gently. Cover and leave to stand for 30 minutes to allow the flavours to be absorbed into the bread.

Lightly mix in the basil then serve drizzled with the remaining olive oil and scattered with the remaining tomato and extra basil leaves.

sheep, dogs and Tuscan cheeses

Many of us who live in sheep-rearing areas outside Italy will not be familiar with the Italian *pecora* or milk-producing sheep. They look very skinny compared to our tubby, woolly breeds. They are creamy white, have long floppy ears, huge dangling oval udders and generally have shorter coats. These Tuscan *pecore* graze on the fragrant meadows of the Apennines, the salty marshes of the Maremma and the lush pastures, nooks and crannies of the Crete Senesi – in fact, anywhere that olives and grapes won't grow.

These wandering, grazing herds are often accompanied by two or three even fluffier 'sheep' with plume-like wagging tails and with more of a deep throaty bark than a sweet little bleat. These are the magnificent and not-to-be-messed-with Maremma sheepdogs or, to be exact, *cane da pastore Maremmano Abruzzese*. There is no shepherd in sight – just a huge flock of sheep, swarming over a swathe of brilliant green grass and two or three of these imposing, cream-coloured, sheep-sized dogs trotting purposefully alongside.

They are guard dogs, not herders, and have been used in Tuscany and Abruzzo for over 2,000 years to guard both sheep and goats. The breed has not changed in all this time. The sheep know that the dogs are there to protect them, and will run to them if they are frightened. The animals are brought up together to establish a bond – the female Maremmas usually giving birth to her puppies in the same place as the sheep, and so the two natural enemies learn to coexist with the help of the shepherd and his family. The dogs are hardy and loyal and their natural instinct is to guard. They can be ferocious, and were originally used to protect the sheep from marauding wolves and bears. In local museums, you can see the frightening heavy leather, metal-spiked collars called *vreccale*, worn to protect their vulnerable throats from the jaws of wild predators. Nowadays, when the sheep need to be milked, the shepherd drives into the pasture in his battered four-by-four or on his quad-bike and drives them back to the milking shed with a dog in front leading the way and one on either side. A word of warning – use a very long lens if you want to photograph the dogs at work; they take the job very seriously indeed!

Ewe's milk is sweet and delicate, and makes the cheese we know today as *pecorino Toscano*. It is the only Tuscan cheese that has been awarded the prestigious mark of the *Denominazione di Origine Protetta (DOP)* (Protected Designation of Origin) out of only 30 awarded throughout Italy. The ancient name for this cheese was *cacio*. I came across a little old lady selling her three best cheeses balanced on a tiny wooden table in the corner of a market. The bottom one was dry and firm, the next was creamier but still firm and nutty and the cheese on the top was making a bid to escape! It was cracking out of its greyish crust, revealing an ooze of creamy yellow. When I asked her what type of cheese it was, she laughed and toothlessly replied, '*cacio!*' Of course. How stupid of me to even enquire. It was just cheese, plain and simple. Sheep farmers had made cheese like this in the area for centuries. But this was her own cheese, made with unpasteurized ewe's milk, and I simply had to buy a big wedge of the ooze, which was coaxed down our throats later with a rush of local Brunello di Montalcino. It was unimaginably good.

There are many varieties of pecorino in Tuscany. The flavour of the cheese depends greatly on the breed of sheep, as well as the type of pasture and soil used for grazing. Ageing affects the flavour and texture, and cheeses range from young and fresh to strong and dry. Tuscan pecorino is not generally used for grating, but eaten with something sweet, such as a perfectly ripe pear or a drizzle of honey. In springtime *cacio marzolino* appears, traditionally the first cheese to curdle in the warming spring air, while immature *pecorini* are eaten with the first tender young broad beans. It is always served very simply so that the complex flavour of the cheese can be enjoyed for itself. Whether pasteurized or not, the milk is heated then coagulated (with rennet) into curds, which are cut and then pressed into moulds to remove the whey. The whey is strained off then reheated to produce *ricotta* (the word literally means recooked), which is not strictly classed as a cheese at all. Ricotta curds are skimmed off and pressed into baskets to drain and the ricotta is ready to use after 3–4 hours. The longer it drains, the firmer and more acidic it becomes. It can also be dry-salted and matured for grating. The softer *pecorini* are then immersed in brine or rubbed with salt and left for up to 8 hours, the harder ones for up to 14. Young *pecorini* are matured for up to 20 days, while the firmer cheeses, called *pecorino stagionato,* are matured for at least 4 months. Cheese pressed the traditional way in woven baskets is called *canestrato*.

Cheese-making in Tuscany has undergone a true renaissance, and highly skilled artisan producers are making incredibly interesting *pecorini*. The most staggering variety I have ever seen was in the town of Pienza. Walk down the main street and your nose will lead you to cheese paradise. There is every size, shape, colour and texture. Outer rinds have been rubbed with tomato and oil, some with wood ash, some with *la morchia* – the dregs from the bottom of olive oil vats – and left to mature. Some are wrapped with leaves, some have nettles or hot red chilli in the paste. All are delicious. You may even cry with the wonder of it all. I did.

Clockwise from top left: Maremma sheepdog; *Pecora* **sheep; Pecorino cheese; Pecorino cheese; lady selling** *cacio* **in a market; Pecorino cheese on sale in a market; cheese and wine shop in Pienza; Pecorino cheeses; Maremma sheepdogs with their herd.**

minestre

soups

the land of the 'bean eaters'

'Fiorentin mangia fagioli, lecapiatti e tovaglioli' goes the saying. Loosely translated, this tells us that Florentines were known as bean eaters and plate and tablecloth-lickers. Not a very complimentary description, but Tuscans do love their beans and also have a reputation for thriftiness. Beans have been cultivated in the region for centuries, the oldest variety being the black-eyed bean, which was known to the ancient Romans and earlier civilizations. In ancient Rome, Pliny the Elder extolled the nutritional value of dried broad beans and the writer Apicius included numerous broad bean recipes in his *'De Re Conquinaria'*, widely regarded as the world's first cookery book. The bean we recognize today as the Tuscan white bean or cannellini bean appeared soon after the discovery of America in 1492. It was highly prized by rich Florentines, who had acquired these new delicacies through trade with Spain and the New World. Due to the ease of cultivation, they soon filtered into the diet of the poor and have remained a staple in Tuscany ever since.

To this day, ordinary dried white beans are called *fagioli di Spagna* (Spanish beans). They tend to be slightly larger than cannellini beans and are eaten fresh out of the pod around July and August. Borlotti beans are beautiful beans marbled with shades of magenta, dark red, cream and white; even the pods are beautiful, and these too are eaten fresh in summertime. Unfortunately, these little works of art turn an even mid-brown colour when cooked, but don't let that put you off, they still taste delicious. The most popular bean is, however, the cannellini, along with the slightly smaller Toscanelli variety (see below), which are high in protein. These varieties have a delicate skin and a mild flavour that makes them a perfect partner to strong-flavoured Tuscan dishes. They were a cheap and sustaining part of a peasant farmer's diet, being packed with slow-release energy for endless toil in the fields.

The cooking of beans has been developed into an art form by the Tuscans. A wonderful Tuscan cook once told me that you will know when the beans are ready because of the 'special smell' that will waft from them. Before the advent of our convenient ovens and hobs, all cooking would have been done in the open fireplace in the kitchen and the simplest method of cooking beans was *Fagioli nel Fiasco* (page 122). Toscanelli beans were used, on account of their small size, and were put in a large Chianti flask with water and a few flavourings. The protective straw covering was removed from the flask and the neck stoppered loosely with a clean rag. The whole thing was buried in the hot embers under the grey ash and left barely to simmer at a constant heat for hours or until the fire went out. Cooked this way, the beans remain whole, but are still soft and creamy inside. It is almost considered a sin to cook beans

to a mush this way. These days, cooking in a terracotta pot or a casserole would work just as well. Beans are not salted as they are cooking, as this can toughen the skins. Some cooks like to add a pinch of bicarbonate of soda to the cooking water to soften the skins and neutralize their sometimes explosive effect.

The best way to eat fresh beans is to boil them lightly and dress them with nothing more than the best extra virgin olive oil and a little salt and freshly ground black pepper. Finely chopped onion is often added to enhance the flavour and it is, in fact, traditional to eat fresh spring onions with a bowl of *La Ribollita* (page 31). *Fagioli all'Uccelletto* (page 121) is probably the most famous bean dish. It literally means 'beans with little birds', but don't look for any small game birds in the beans. All birds and wildlife were once the prerogative of rich landowners, so the country dwellers made the dish with beans and the flavourings that went with the game birds, with some fresh sausage if there was any to hand. This dish became a firm part of Tuscan *cucina povera* (poor man's cooking). Beans, chickpeas and lentils appear in every aspect of Tuscan cooking, from antipasti and crostini, to soups and *contorni* (vegetable side dishes).

Almost everywhere you shop for food in Tuscany you will find packets of a wheat-like grain called *farro*, which has become tremendously popular over the years. The wholegrain is used to make all manner of salads and soups, such as *Minestra di Farro* (page 39), a type of risotto called *farrotto,* and even desserts. It is an unhybridized European ancestor of modern wheat with a hearty, nutty flavour and a chewy texture. A good source of protein, *farro* also contains high levels of Vitamin E and fibre. According to legend, it is a form of natural viagra, if tales from the people of Garfagnana are to be believed!

Polenta (maize meal or cornmeal) is really a Northern Italian staple, but it is also popular in Tuscany due to its suitability for the hearty soups and stews. In times gone by, it would have been a staple of the poor and farming communities. Polenta is ground from dried maize and can be fine (soft polenta), coarse (thick set polenta) or a blend of the two. It is usually golden yellow in colour, but it can be made from white maize kernels. It is sometimes mixed with wheat flour to make bread, such as *La Marocca* (page 52), but is traditionally cooked with water and salt to make a thick porridge-like dish. I would not recommend instant or quick-cook polenta as the taste and texture is all wrong, and can put you off polenta for life!

Clockwise from top left: Toscanelli beans in a chianti flask; chickpeas, borlotti beans, *farro*, cannellini beans, black-eyed beans and green lentils; broad bean pods; a field of broad beans.

I know I am truly back in Tuscany when I see *cavolo nero* (Tuscan black winter cabbage) growing in rows in small allotments, looking like mini palm trees. Savoy cabbage makes a good alternative, however. This basic bean and vegetable soup is usually made one day, then reheated the next, when the flavours will have really developed. It is ladled over toasted garlic bread, trickled with olive oil and served with lots of Parmesan cheese. This is the perfect soup for a big family get-together, best made in quantity, and is very filling. *Ribollita* literally means 'reboiled' and is made from whatever vegetables are around, but must contain beans and the delicious *cavolo nero*.

la ribollita

250 g dried cannellini beans
150 ml extra virgin olive oil
1 onion, finely chopped
1 carrot, chopped
1 celery stick, chopped
2 leeks, finely chopped
4 garlic cloves, finely chopped
1 small Dutch (white) cabbage, shredded
1 large potato, peeled and chopped
4 medium courgettes, chopped
400 ml Italian sieved tomatoes *(passata)*
2 sprigs fresh rosemary
2 sprigs fresh thyme
2 sprigs fresh sage
1 whole dried red chilli
500 g cavolo nero (Tuscan black winter cabbage) or savoy cabbage, finely shredded
sea salt and freshly ground black pepper

to serve
6 thick slices coarse crusty white bread
1 garlic clove, peeled and bruised
extra virgin olive oil
freshly grated Parmesan cheese

serves 8

Soak the cannellini beans overnight in plenty of cold water.

Heat half the olive oil in a heavy stockpot and add the onion, carrot and celery. Cook gently for about 10 minutes, stirring frequently. Next add the leeks and garlic and cook for another 10 minutes. Add the Dutch cabbage, potato and courgettes, stir well and cook for 10 minutes, stirring frequently. Stir in the soaked beans, passata, rosemary, thyme and sage, dried chilli, salt and plenty of black pepper. Cover with about 2 litres water (the vegetables should be well-covered), bring to the boil, then turn down the heat and simmer, covered, for at least 2 hours, until the beans are very soft.

Transfer 2–3 large ladlefuls of soup to a bowl and mash well using the back of the ladle. Return to the soup to thicken it. Stir in the cavolo nero and simmer for another 15 minutes. Allow to cool then refrigerate overnight.

The next day, slowly reheat the soup and stir in the remaining olive oil. Toast the bread and rub with garlic. Arrange the bread over the base of a tureen or individual bowls and ladle the soup over it. Trickle with extra olive oil and serve with plenty of Parmesan.

rice and fresh bean soup
minestra di riso con fagioli

This lovely soup is made with fresh white beans in season and dried white beans in winter. In summer it is sometimes served at room temperature or chilled. The combination of rice and fresh beans make this much lighter than other Tuscan soups. You could even substitute *farro* for rice.

800 g fresh white beans, in the pod

3 tablespoons olive oil

50 g Italian dry-cured ham (*prosciutto crudo*), finely chopped

1 onion, finely chopped

1 stick celery, finely chopped

1 garlic clove, finely chopped

a pinch of dried chilli flakes

500 g ripe red tomatoes, skinned, deseeded and chopped or 400 g can chopped tomatoes

1 tablespoon chopped fresh basil leaves

200 g rice

sea salt and freshly ground black pepper

2 tablespoons finely shredded basil leaves, to garnish

serves 4

Pod the beans and put them into a saucepan, covering them with 2 litres cold water. Bring to the boil then simmer gently for 15–20 minutes until tender.

Meanwhile, heat the oil in a smaller saucepan then add the ham, onion, celery, garlic and chilli flakes. Cook for a few minutes until the onion is golden and translucent. Add the tomatoes and basil, stir well, then simmer for 15 minutes.

Add the sauce and the rice to the beans and their water and stir well. Season with salt and pepper. Bring to the boil, then simmer gently for about 15 minutes until the rice is tender. Serve piping hot sprinkled with the shredded basil.

chestnut and pancetta soup
minestra di castagne e pancetta

I made this robust and chunky soup after gathering fresh sweet chestnuts with Italian friends in the Chianti hills one October afternoon. Preparing the chestnuts is a bit of a chore, but the flavour and texture is wonderful! Use dried chestnuts at a pinch (available from good delicatessens and Italian stores), or soaked dried chickpeas. Make sure the chestnuts are no more than 1 year old as they can go stale. This soup has a surprisingly sweet taste so you can add a dash of lemon juice, if you like.

750 g fresh, plump, sweet chestnuts or 400 g dried chestnuts, soaked overnight in cold water

125 g butter

150 g pancetta or streaky bacon, diced

2 medium onions, finely chopped

1 carrot, finely chopped

1 celery stick, finely chopped

1 tablespoon chopped fresh rosemary

2 fresh bay leaves

2 garlic cloves, halved

sea salt and freshly ground black pepper

serves 6

Using a small sharp knife, slit the shell of each chestnut across the rounded side. Put the chestnuts in a saucepan and cover with cold water. Bring to the boil and simmer for 15–20 minutes. Remove from the heat and lift out a few chestnuts. Peel off the outer thick skin, then peel away the inner thinner skin (this has a bitter taste). Alternatively roast the chestnuts in a preheated oven at 200°C (400°F) Gas 6 for 15 minutes, then peel off the skins.

Melt the butter in a large saucepan and add the pancetta. Fry over a medium heat until the fat begins to run. Add the onions, carrot and celery and cook for 5–10 minutes until beginning to soften and brown. Add the chestnuts to the pan with the rosemary, bay leaves, garlic and enough water to cover completely. Bring to the boil, half cover, turn down the heat and simmer for 30–45 minutes, stirring occasionally, until the chestnuts start to disintegrate and thicken the soup. Taste and season well with salt and pepper.

A light fresh soup of courgettes and clams called *aquacotta* or 'cooked water'. This is a very simple soup, made more substantial by ladling over toasted bread as would be done in the country, to take the edge off your appetite. This is a light summery soup from coastal Tuscany. Many versions are made according to what is available – for example, *Aquacotta di Monte* might have porcini mushrooms and a bit of sausage in it. Farm workers cooked this in a bucket over a fire when out working in the fields, adding whatever was to hand. *Nepitella* is a wild herb much like catmint, and grows abundantly in Tuscany.

summer clam & courgette soup
aquacotta di mare

750 g fresh baby clams or cockles in shell, cleaned

3 tablespoons extra virgin olive oil

1 large garlic clove, finely chopped

750 g courgettes, roughly grated

finely grated zest and freshly squeezed juice of 1 unwaxed lemon

1 tablespoon chopped fresh marjoram, oregano or nepitella

1 litre vegetable stock or water

4 thick slices country bread, toasted

1 large garlic clove, peeled and bruised

extra virgin olive oil, to drizzle

sea salt and freshly ground black pepper

serves 4

Put the clams in a saucepan and set over a high heat. Cover and cook for a few minutes until they open. Take off the heat, tip into a colander placed over a bowl to catch the juices. Reserve the juice and remove half the clams from their shells, keeping the remaining clams in their shells.

Heat the olive oil in the same saucepan and add the garlic. Cook gently until golden but not brown. Add the courgettes, lemon zest and marjoram and turn in the oil and garlic until coated. Pour in the stock, season lightly and bring to simmering point, cover and simmer for about 10 minutes or until the courgettes are cooked. Add the reserved clam juices and the reserved clam meat. Taste and season with salt and pepper, and lemon juice to taste. Gently stir in the reserved clams in their shells and heat through.

To serve, rub the toasted bread with garlic, place a slice in each bowl and ladle on the soup. Drizzle each serving with olive oil and serve immediately.

creamy tomato and bread soup with basil oil
pappa al pomodoro

***Pappa al pomodoro* is only as good as its ingredients –** great tomatoes, good bread and wonderful, green olive oil. This is one of the most comforting soups on earth and, as you might expect, has its origins in peasant thriftiness. Leftover bread is never thrown away in Tuscany as there is always a use for it. Here it thickens a rich tomato soup, which is in turn enriched with Parmesan – a nod to modern tastes as an aged local pecorino would traditionally have been used. You will see this soup on every menu around Florence, Siena and Arezzo, but it is hard to find a good one. My addition is the flavoured oil – in Tuscany you would be given extra virgin olive oil to pour over the soup.

1.5 litres vegetable, chicken or meat stock
4 tablespoons extra virgin olive oil
1 onion, peeled and chopped
1.2 kg very ripe, soft tomatoes, chopped
300 g stale white bread, crusts removed and thinly sliced or made into breadcrumbs
3 cloves garlic, peeled and crushed
125 g freshly grated Parmesan, plus extra to serve

basil and rocket oil
150 ml extra virgin olive oil
3 tablespoons chopped fresh basil
3 tablespoons chopped fresh rocket
sea salt and freshly ground black pepper

serves 6

Heat the stock slowly in a large saucepan. Meanwhile, heat the oil in a large saucepan and add the onion and tomatoes and fry over a gentle heat for 10 minutes until soft. Push the mixture through a food mill, mouli or sieve, and stir into the stock. Add the bread and garlic. Cover and simmer gently for about 45 minutes until thick and creamy, giving a good whisk every now and then to break up the bread. Watch out, as this soup can catch on the bottom.

Meanwhile, to make the basil and rocket oil, process the olive oil, basil and rocket in a blender until completely smooth and pour through a fine strainer, if necessary. Stir the Parmesan into the soup and season with salt and pepper to taste. Ladle into bowls and trickle with 2 tablespoons basil and rocket oil and serve hot, warm or cold (but never chilled). Serve extra Parmesan separately.

Italian *farro* is a very ancient grain, originally cultivated by the Romans until wheat overtook it in popularity. *Farro* (botanical name, *Triticum spelta*), is a close relation of the grain spelt and is enjoying a renaissance in Tuscany and Umbria, where it is grown in the Lucca and Garfagnana areas. In Tuscany, it is cooked with beans to make a creamy, nutty soup. Like most soups in this area, it is traditionally served poured over thick slices of country bread.

creamy wheat and bean soup with rosemary
minestra di farro

250 g Italian *farro* or whole spelt grains

300 g dried borlotti beans

100 g dried chickpeas

a pinch of bicarbonate of soda

6 tablespoons extra virgin olive oil, plus extra to drizzle

2 garlic cloves, finely chopped

2 tablespoons chopped fresh rosemary

1 tablespoon tomato purée diluted with 100 ml warm water

sea salt and freshly ground black pepper

serves 6

Soak the beans and the chickpeas overnight in abundant cold water. Drain, then cook with a pinch of bicarbonate of soda in a large pan of boiling water for 45 minutes to 1 hour until tender. Drain, reserving 2 litres of the cooking water. Mash the beans a little to start them disintegrating, then set aside.

Heat the oil in a medium saucepan and add the garlic and rosemary. Cook for 1 minute until the garlic turns light golden and the rosemary releases its fragrance. Add the diluted tomato purée, then pour in the reserved cooking water. Bring to the boil, then stir in the *farro*. Season with salt and pepper and simmer gently for 1 hour or until the *farro* is *al dente*. Stir in the lightly mashed bean mixture. Taste and adjust the seasoning, being generous with the pepper. Reheat, adding extra water if the soup is too thick. Serve in large bowls with extra virgin olive oil to drizzle over the top.

On every fish stall in Italy you will see a box of small bony fish marked *per zuppa* – 'for soup'. These fish haven't much flesh but have a lot of bone, which helps to make a great-tasting fish broth. *Cacciucco* should have 5 or 6 varieties of fish, including squid and octopus. The fish have wonderful names like *capone gallinella* (tub gurnard), *scorfano* (scorpion fish), *tracina* (weever), *palombetto* (dogfish), *scoglio* and *cicale* (mantis shrimp). Unlike most fish soups, there are no bones in this. This soup was born out of poverty and is what the fishermen might cook for themselves after they have sold the best of the catch. It is best washed down with a young and robust red wine.

livornese fish stew
il cacciucco alla livornese

750 g mixed bony fish, such as tub gurnard, scorpion fish or weever

500 g dogfish or monkfish, skinned

500 g squid or octopus, cleaned

500 g clams or mussels, cleaned (page 89)

500 g mantis shrimp or Dublin bay prawns

6 tablespoons extra virgin olive oil

1 onion, finely chopped

2 garlic cloves, finely chopped

1 dried red chilli, finely chopped

150 ml dry white wine

6 ripe red tomatoes, skinned, deseeded and chopped or 600 g canned chopped tomatoes

a little hot fish stock or water (optional)

6 slices stale bread, toasted

1 garlic clove, bruised

sea salt and freshly ground black pepper

chopped fresh parsley, to garnish

serves 6

First prepare the fish or ask the fishmonger to do this for you. Wash all the fish, scale them, gut them and trim off the fins. Cut the dogfish into large chunks. To prepare the squid, rinse it well. Hold the body in one hand and firmly pull the tentacles with the other, to remove the soft contents of the body pouch. Cut the tentacles just in front of the eyes and discard the body contents, reserve the tentacles. Rinse the body pouches under cold running water then slice into rings. To prepare the octopus, cut off the tentacles near the head. Pop out the 'beak' then cut above the eyes and discard them. Turn the body inside out and remove the entrails. Pound the body and tentacles with a meat mallet until tender. Set aside with the squid.

Heat the olive oil in a wide shallow saucepan, add the onion, garlic and chilli and cook for a few minutes until golden. Add the wine and bubble until the wine evaporates. Add the squid and octopus and stir-fry for 1–2 minutes, then add the tomatoes, season with salt and pepper, and simmer for about 15 minutes. Add the fish and mantis shrimp, cover and cook for 15 minutes, without stirring. Add the clams and cook for 5 minutes, without stirring. You may like to add a little hot stock to keep it moist. Rub the toasted bread with the garlic and lay each slice on the base of a soup bowl. Ladle the fish and cooking liquor over the toast and serve sprinkled with parsley.

pane e pasta

bread and pizza
pasta, risotto and gnocchi

bread and salt

Pane sciocco (Tuscan bread) has been made without salt for centuries and is an integral part of Tuscan cuisine. For those not familiar with it, the taste can be something of a disappointment. There are no two ways about it, it is truly bland and it takes some persuasion to acquire a taste for it. However, it is this very blandness that lets the highly seasoned flavours of the local hams, salamis and cured meats shine through. The bread is the carrier of the flavour, whether as the base of crostini or bruschetta, in soups like *Pappa al Pomodoro* (page 36) and *La Ribollita* (page 31), in the summer salad *Panzanella* (page 23), or as a crisp component of a meat kebab. It is never thrown out by the thrifty Tuscans – if it goes stale, it will be dried and made into breadcrumbs. Even I, a big salt fan, have been converted, and love it toasted for breakfast and spread with white Italian butter and homemade jam. In fact, I like it so much now, that I have developed a simple recipe (page 46) to make at home in Scotland whenever I have a pang for it, and I must say it works very well indeed.

The bread is so particular to the region, that it has been given a *Denominazione di Origine Protetta (DOP)* (Protected Designation of Origin). The real stuff to look for is *Pane Toscano a Lievitazione Naturale* – Tuscan bread made by natural fermentation – marked *Consorzio di Promozione e Tutela (CTP).* This mark or brand has to follow very strict rules of production, unlike supermarkets and non-artisan bakers who produce bread made without salt, but not with the special flavours of natural yeasts and artisan flours captured in hand-made breads cooked in wood-fired ovens.

Making bread with natural yeast takes longer, but the bread will have more flavour, will keep longer and is easier to digest. Real Tuscan bread can be kept for up to a week – a tradition stemming from the country practice of baking a huge batch of bread once a week in a wood-fired oven which was then wrapped in a cloth and stored in a cupboard to last until next baking day. The main shape is the round loaf called the *bozza*, the long *filone* and long flattish *ciabatta*. The crust is rustic, crunchy, a mid-brown colour and the white crumb unevenly honeycombed with tiny air bubbles due to the slow rising which the dough is given. Ideally, it is best cooked in a wood-fired oven, but these are increasingly rare in Tuscany. The flavour of bread cooked in a wood-fired oven is exquisite, and well worth seeking out.

The most common Tuscan breads are *pane Toscano*, made with natural yeast and a mixture of 0 and 00 flours and water; and *pane integrale*, which is made with natural yeast and a mixture of 100% wholemeal flour ground from both soft and hard wheat and water. *Pane casareccio* or *semi-integrale* is made with natural yeast, and a mixture of 0 or 00 flour, Type 2 and 1 unrefined flours, wholemeal *farro*, barley flour, wheatgerm, bran and water. There are also many other types of flavoured breads containing nuts, seeds, spices, different flours and even chocolate, which are specialities of particular bakers.

Some terms used in Italian Breadmaking

Lievito madre: literally the mother yeast or starter, usually a piece of dough kept back from a batch or a piece of cooked bread.

Biga: the biga is the fermented paste of natural yeast, made using the mother yeast (see above) with added flour and water used as the base to make the final bread dough.

Madia: a type of wooden chest which was used to make bread dough and store flour, yeast and other breadmaking ingredients. They are much sought-after antiques nowadays.

Pane raffermo: stale bread

Pane sciocco: saltless bread. *Sciocco* is the term used in Tuscany for a food made without salt.

Although bread is made without salt in Tuscany, it is impossible to imagine Tuscan cuisine without the pungency of salt, which can be a bit overpowering if you're not used to it! Since antiquity, salt has been a valuable economic, medicinal and culinary commodity all around the world. Many modern Italian and English words have their roots in the Latin word for salt: *sal*. 'Salary', for example, comes from the Latin phrase *salarium argentum* (salt money) which referred to part of the payment made to every Roman soldier who worked on building the Via Salaria, or Salt Road, between the salt works at Ostia and the city of Rome, eventually linking Rome with Sabina on the Adriatic coast.

Papal efforts to impose a salt tax in Tuscany in the 16th century resulted in the fiercely independent and defiant Tuscans refusing to put salt in their bread – a custom which they still maintain to this day. Until as late as 1975, the manufacture and sale of salt was a state monopoly in Italy, the government fixing the market price, which included a tax rate of about 70%. There were discount rates for agricultural and industrial use, and its production was tax free in Sicily and Sardinia. Salt could only be sold from shops displaying the '*Sali e Tabacchi*' sign (see opposite). Italian salt is mainly produced from evaporation of Mediterranean sea water in coastal salt flats or lagoons. Much is imported from the ancient salt flats in Sicily, and has a high mineral content. It is available as *sale fino*, a finely ground sea salt used in baking and as table salt, and *sale grosso*, a coarse sea salt used for salting cooking water for pasta and vegetables, and for curing meat.

Clockwise from top: wheat field; salt and tobacco sign; homemade Tuscan saltless bread.

tuscan saltless bread
pane toscano

Tuscans like heavily seasoned food, but not their bread. It is said that as salt used to be taxed, it was not added to a daily necessity like bread, but kept for preserving meat, vegetables and fish. I find that it complements Tuscan food very well and is the perfect vehicle for dipping into olive oil as it doesn't compete for taste. This recipe uses a *biga*, or *madre*, as a starter, to give the bread a more genuine, slightly sourdough taste. It is easy to make and once you've tried it, you'll never make bread any other way! Using this starter gives the pleasant slightly sour taste so characteristic of country breads.

biga

150 ml warm water

1 tablespoon dried active yeast

115 g plain unbleached flour, warmed*

bread dough

about 200 ml warm* water

400 g plain unbleached flour, warmed*, plus extra, for kneading and shaping

makes one 600 g loaf

To make the biga, pour the warm water into a medium bowl and whisk in the yeast until dissolved, then gradually whisk in all the flour to form a smooth loose batter.

Transfer the biga to a large bowl and whisk in the warm water. Now mix in the flour gradually until you have a pliable, firm dough (err on the soft side rather than have it too firm). Gather it together in the bowl, making sure all the flour is kneaded in. Lift out onto a clean floured work surface and knead for 10 minutes. The dough will be a bit stickier than normal, so keep flouring your hands, but not the table or the dough as you don't want to change the proportions. When the dough begins to become very elastic, it is ready to shape. With one hand, pull the outside edge towards the middle, turning the dough as you go round to form a ball. Flip over onto some flour then pull gently to form a rough rectangle. Flip this over again onto a floured baking sheet so that the rough side is uppermost. Cover with a large upturned bowl and leave to rise until almost doubled – about 1½ hours.

Put a roasting tin of hot water on the base of a preheated oven. Bake the loaf at 200°C (400°F) Gas 6 for 35–40 minutes until it sounds hollow when tapped on the underside. Cool on a wire rack. The bread will freeze for up to 3 months.

*Note Warm means blood temperature. You should be able to hold your finger in the water without any pain! Warming the flour speeds up the reaction of the yeast. You can do this in the microwave. Put the flour in a non-metallic bowl and cook on HIGH for 20 seconds. Remove from the microwave and fluff up the flour with your fingers – it should feel warm – if not, return it to the oven for another 10 seconds or so. Use it before it cools, but don't use it if it is too hot as it may kill the yeast.

Originally these rosemary-flavoured buns were prepared on *Giovedì Santo* (Maundy Thursday), but now they are eaten all year round, especially in Florence. The cuts in the top of these fragrant Florentine buns represent the Cross, but are also made to enable a better rise. The olive oil is essential for a good flavour, so use the best. Although raisins are traditional, I sometimes add chopped ready-to-eat figs which make a delicious alternative. These make a nice change from hot cross buns at Easter.

rosemary, sultana and olive oil bread
pandiramerino

1 tablespoon dried active yeast

3 tablespoons caster sugar

400 g plain white flour, warmed (page 46)

2 large sprigs fresh rosemary

6 tablespoons extra virgin olive oil

150 g sultanas, raisins or dried muscatel grapes

makes 6–8 rolls

Dissolve the yeast and 1 teaspoon of the sugar in 250 ml warm water and leave to stand for 10 minutes until frothy.

Sift the flour into a bowl, add the remaining sugar, then make a well in the centre and add the yeast liquid. Mix until it comes together, then knead on a lightly floured work surface for 10 minutes until elastic. Put the dough in a clean bowl, cover with clingfilm and leave to rise in a warm place for about 1½ hours.

Meanwhile, wash and dry the rosemary and strip off the leaves. Lightly bruise them with the end of a rolling pin. Heat 4 tablespoons of the olive oil and the bruised rosemary leaves in a small saucepan. Remove from the heat and allow to cool. Strain when cold.

Uncover the dough and knock it back. Tip out onto the work surface and knead the cooled olive oil and rosemary into the dough with the sultanas. Divide the dough into 6 pieces and shape each one into a neat round ball, then put on a floured baking sheet and flatten slightly. Using a very sharp knife, make two long vertical cuts in the top of each roll, followed by two horizontal ones, like a grid. Cover and leave to rise in a warm place for 30–40 minutes until doubled in size.

Uncover the dough, then brush lightly with the remaining flavoured olive oil. Bake in a preheated oven at 180°C (350°F) Gas 4 for about 30 minutes until risen and brown, and it sounds hollow when tapped on the bottom.

Schiacciate (skee-a-chah-tay) in Tuscany are individual thin crispy pizzas with the simplest of toppings. Forget Neapolitan pizzas – the dough is rolled out to almost paper thinness, laid on an oiled tray, then topped with wafer-thin slices of cheese, vegetables and prosciutto, all of which is cut incredibly thinly so that it will cook quickly. Mozzarella is often used as the base instead of tomato sauce, and sliced fresh tomatoes or halved cherry tomatoes are scattered on top of the cheese. Fresh herbs or a handful of peppery rocket are added when the pizza comes sizzling out of the oven. Good topping combinations include aubergine, red onions, mozzarella and sage; potato, anchovy and sage or rosemary, olives and mozzarella; courgette, mozzarella, anchovy and basil; and mozzarella, tomato and rocket.

little tuscan pizzas
schiacciate

15 g fresh yeast, 1 tablespoon dried active yeast or 1 sachet fast-action dried yeast

a pinch of sugar

250 ml warm water

350 g plain white flour

about 200 ml extra virgin olive oil

½ teaspoon salt

thinly sliced mozzarella, tomatoes, prosciutto, red onion, aubergine, potato or courgette

a selection of anchovy fillets, capers or stoned black olives

fine cornmeal, to sprinkle

fresh basil, sage or rocket leaves, to serve

makes 6

To make the pizza dough, cream the fresh yeast with the sugar in a small bowl, then whisk in the warm water. Leave for 10 minutes until frothy. if using dried yeast, follow the manufacturer's instructions. Sift the flour into a large bowl and make a well in the centre. Pour in the yeast mixture, 1 tablespoon olive oil and the salt. Mix together with a round-bladed knife, then using hands until the dough comes together. Tip out onto a floured surface. With clean, dry hands, knead the dough for 10 minutes until smooth, elastic and quite soft. If it is too soft to handle, knead in a little more flour. Put in a clean oiled bowl, cover with a damp tea towel and leave to rise for about 1 hour until doubled in size.

Uncover the dough and knock it back, divide into 6 balls and roll each one into a very thin circle. Put on a couple of baking sheets sprinkled with fine cornmeal. Toss the sliced vegetables in a little olive oil and arrange sparingly on top of the disks along with your choice of anchovies, capers and olives. Season well and drizzle with more olive oil, then bake in a preheated oven at 230°C (450°F) Gas 8 for 15–20 minutes until golden and crisp. Scatter with herbs, drizzle with olive oil and serve immediately.

olive and cornmeal focaccia with rosemary and sage
la marocca

An unusual bread from the coastal areas of Lunigiana made from a mixture of cornmeal and wheat flour. It is made between November and the end of January to coincide with the olive harvest. It was traditionally cooked in a wood-fired oven on a bed of chestnut leaves, and took on a deep brown crust – it is thought that its name refers to the dark skin of Morroccan sea traders. In fact throughout Tuscany, there are many breads and rolls with dark crusts called *Marocca*, *Pan Maroko* or *Morocca*. A little chilli, chopped rosemary, sage and garlic are often added. It must be eaten on the day, and is often served as part of an antipasto.

500 g plain flour
300 g fine polenta flour (*farina gialla* or *granoturco*)
2 sachets fast-action dried yeast
200 g black olives, stoned and halved
a few rosemary sprigs
2 tablespoons sage, chopped
2–3 garlic cloves, finely chopped
50 g pine nuts (optional)
3 tablespoons extra virgin olive oil, plus extra for drizzling
salt crystals and freshly ground black pepper

a 33 x 23 cm Swiss roll tin

makes one 33 x 23 cm focaccia

Mix the two flours and yeast in a large bowl. Add the olives, herbs, garlic and pine nuts, if using and mix to coat. Make a well in the centre and add the olive oil mixed with about 200 ml warm water. Mix to a soft dough and knead lightly.

Turn the dough out onto a floured board. Roll out into a rectangle to fit the Swiss roll tin. Cover and leave to rise in a warm place for about 20 minutes until slightly puffy. Make dimples all over the dough with your fingers and drizzle with olive oil. Sprinkle with salt crystals and bake in preheated oven at 200°C (400°F) Gas 6 for about 35 minutes until risen, firm and dark golden brown.

thick focaccia
focaccia

750 g Italian 00 flour or plain white flour, plus extra as necessary

½ teaspoon fine sea salt

25 g fresh yeast, 1 tablespoon dried active yeast or 1 sachet fast-action dried yeast

150 ml extra virgin olive oil

coarse sea salt or crystal salt

two 25 cm cake tins, pie or pizza plates

makes two 25 cm focaccias

Focaccia literally means a bread that was baked on the hearth, but is easy to bake in conventional ovens. It is found in many different forms, and can be thin and crisp, thick and soft, or round or square. I make this one in a tin, but it can be formed into any shape you wish and cooked on a baking tray. A terracotta bakestone or unglazed terracotta floor tile heated in the oven will give pizzas and focaccia extra lift and a crisp base. Although a rustic focaccia can be made with any basic pizza dough, the secret of a truly light thick focaccia lies in three risings, and dimpling the dough so that it traps olive oil while it bakes.

Sift the flour with the fine salt into a large bowl and make a well in the centre. Crumble in the yeast, or add dried yeast, if using. If using dried active yeast, follow the manufacturer's instructions. Pour in 3 tablespoons olive oil, then rub in the yeast until the mixture resembles fine breadcrumbs. Pour in 450 ml warm water and mix together with your hands until the dough comes together. Tip the dough out onto a floured surface, wash and dry your hands and knead for 10 minutes until smooth and elastic. The dough should be quite soft, but if it is too soft to handle, add more flour. Put in an oiled bowl, cover with a damp tea towel and leave to rise in a warm place until doubled – about 1½ hours.

Lightly oil two shallow 25 cm cake tins, pie or pizza plates. Uncover the dough and knock it back, then divide in two. Shape each into a round ball on a floured surface and roll out into two 25 cm circles and place in the tins. Cover with a damp tea towel and leave to rise for 30 minutes. Remove the tea towel and using your finger tips, make dimples all over the surface of the dough. They can be quite deep. Drizzle over the remaining oil, cover again and leave to rise for a final 30 minutes.

Spray with water, and sprinkle generously with salt, and bake in a preheated oven at 200°C (400°F) Gas 6 for 20–25 minutes until risen and golden brown. Transfer to a wire rack to cool. Eat the same day or freeze immediately.

Variation To make *schiacciata croccante* – thin, crisp focaccia – knead 2 teaspoons chopped fresh rosemary into the dough. After rising, divide into 6 and roll out until 2.5 mm thick. Press onto oiled baking sheets, brush with olive oil, scatter with coarse salt and bake at 230°C (450°F) Gas 8 for 8 minutes.

Cecina is found in pizzerias in north-western Tuscany in Versilia, Massa Carrara, Lunigiana, Livorno, Lucca and Pisa. It is variously described as *Torta di Ceci*, or just *Torta*, and *Focaccia ai Ceci*. It is traditionally baked in a large, shallow copper pan, but a wide metal pizza pan will do instead. It is eaten as an appetizer and can be flavoured with chopped rosemary, dried chilli or black pepper. Sometimes the batter is left to stand overnight to improve the flavour. I love it. If you can't find Italian chickpea flour, use gram flour which is available in Asian food stores.

chickpea flatbread
cecìna

500 ml water

4 tablespoons extra virgin olive oil

200 g Italian chickpea flour or gram flour

½–1 teaspoon sea salt, plus extra for sprinkling

freshly ground black pepper

a 28 cm round pizza pan

makes one 28 cm flatbread

Put the water in a bowl with 1 tablespoon of the oil and gradually whisk in the chickpea flour and salt until smooth and creamy. Cover and leave to stand for at least 30 minutes.

Swirl the remaining olive oil around the base and sides of a 28 cm round pizza pan, preferably non-stick. It must look oily to give the right flavour and crisp edge. Give the batter a stir and pour into the pan. Bake in a preheated oven at 220°C (425°F) Gas 7 or hotter, if possible, for about 20 minutes or until set and golden brown. Serve warm, sprinkled with salt and pepper.

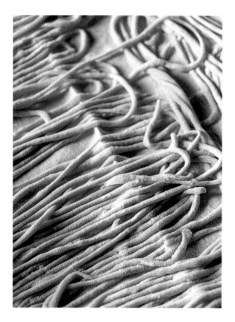

Also known as *pinci*, this hand-rolled spaghetti originates from Val d'Orcia in the Siena region, and the best is said to come from Montalcino. I was inspired to make them after eating them in a campsite restaurant outside Assisi, of all places. They are usually served with a rich meat sauce, often containing dried porcini mushrooms. In Tuscany, they are still made at home for special occasions. As they are so labour intensive, I would only ever make them for very special friends and with time on my hands. The dough contains no eggs, only flour, water and olive oil.

tuscan hand-rolled pasta
pici

Sift the flour into a bowl with a good pinch of salt. Make a well in the centre and add about 150 ml water and the olive oil. Mix this together with a blunt knife until it starts to come together. Try to incorporate all the flour into the dough. If it feels dry, then add a splash more water. If it feels too wet, add a sprinkling of flour. Tip out onto a floured work surface and knead until smooth for 5 minutes. Place in a plastic bag and rest the dough at room temperature for 30 minutes.

Roll the dough out to a thickness of ½ cm and not more than 10 cm wide. Cut into ½ cm wide strips, 20 cm long. Lightly oil your hands, then roll each strip of pasta on a lightly floured surface as if it was a rolling pin, until about 20.5 cm long. Put them on a floured tea towel and roll the rest of the strips in the same way. Drop into a large pan of boiling salted water, stir well and bring back to the boil. Once boiling again, boil for 1 minute. Drain, reserving 1 tablespoon of the cooking water. Mix with the sauce and serve in warm bowls with plenty of freshly grated Parmesan.

500 g plain white flour or Italian 00 flour, plus extra as necessary
1 tablespoon olive oil
sea salt
1 recipe *Sugo Toscano di Carne* (page 72)
freshly grated Parmesan cheese, to serve

serves 4–6

salt cod ravioli with tomatoes
ravioli di baccalà con pomodori

There are two types of dried cod used in Italy – *baccalà* (salted and dried cod) and *stoccafisso* (simply, dried cod and confusingly called *baccalà* by Venetians). Needless to say, Tuscans use the salted dried cod which is often sold ready-soaked (*baccalà ammollato*). Salt cod has a wonderful fresh taste, and if properly soaked (for at least 24 hours) is not too salty. To make it at home, put 500 g fresh skinned cod fillet in a non-corrosive container. Cover completely with a layer of fine sea salt, cover with clingfilm and leave in the refrigerator for at least 4 hours. After this time, all the salt will have dissolved and drawn the moisture out of the fish, and it will be sitting in a watery brine. Drain, rinse and use as directed.

300 g plain white flour or Italian 00 flour

3 eggs

1 tablespoon extra virgin olive oil, plus extra to serve

250 g medium potatoes, peeled

3–4 garlic cloves, peeled

250 g pre-soaked boneless salt cod

100 ml extra virgin olive oil

2 tablespoons chopped fresh parsley

sea salt and freshly ground pepper

tomato sauce

4 tablespoons olive oil

350 g cherry tomatoes, halved

2 tablespoons chopped fresh basil, plus extra leaves to serve

serves 4

To make the pasta dough, sift the flour and a large pinch of salt onto a clean work surface and make a well in the centre with your fist. Beat the eggs and olive oil together and pour into the well. Gradually mix the eggs into the flour with the fingers of one hand and bring it together into a dough. Knead the dough until smooth, lightly massage with a hint of olive oil, put in a plastic bag and allow to rest for at least 30 minutes

Meanwhile, make the filling. Boil the potatoes and garlic for 20 minutes until tender. Rinse the salt cod and poach in simmering water for 10 minutes until it flakes easily. Drain, remove any skin or bones, then flake. Mash the potatoes and garlic, then beat in the fish alternately with the olive oil. Add the parsley, taste and season with salt and pepper. Transfer to a piping bag with a 1.25 cm plain piping tube.

Cut the pasta dough into 4 pieces and roll each piece into a thin sheet. If using a pasta machine, roll to the penultimate setting. Lay a piece of pasta on a lightly floured work surface and cover the other pieces with clingfilm. Pipe small mounds of filling, about 3 cm wide, in even rows at 4 cm intervals across the dough. Brush the spaces of dough between the mounds with water, being careful not to wet the work surface or the dough may stick. Using a rolling pin, lift the remaining sheet of pasta over the top and press down firmly between the mounds of filling, to expel any air bubbles. Cut into rectangles with a ravioli cutter or sharp knife. Alternatively, stamp into rounds, pipe the filling on top, then fold into half moons and seal the edges. Transfer to a lightly floured tea towel. Repeat with the remaining filling and dough.

To make the sauce, heat the olive oil until almost smoking, add the tomatoes and cook over a high heat for 2–3 minutes. Season and add the basil. Bring a large saucepan of salted water to the boil and cook the ravioli for 3 minutes until puffy. Drain well and toss with a little olive oil. Serve with the tomato sauce and extra basil leaves.

wide egg noodles with rich hare sauce
pappardelle alla lepre

This really rich, wintry sauce is legendary in Tuscany, the land of the hunter. I try to make it every year in my cookery classes if we can persuade a local hunter to bag a hare or two. The meat is rich and flavoursome, and tastes of the wild. Hares are not the nicest of things to prepare, so use rubber gloves – it's really worth the work, as the resulting sauce is fabulous! Use rabbit for a much lighter sauce, or even duck. Traditionally the meat is cooked on the bone then the bones are removed and the flesh pulled into shreds. The texture is an acquired taste, so I remove the bones first, keeping the bones for making a stock.

1 medium hare, skinned and jointed (1 farmed rabbit or two small wild rabbits, or 4 small duck breasts)

3 tablespoons olive oil

4 tablespoons butter

1 onion, finely diced

1 carrot, finely diced

1 stick of celery, finely diced

2 garlic cloves, chopped

75 g unsmoked pancetta, finely diced

2 tablespoons flour

300 ml dry red wine

about 600 ml game or good-quality chicken stock

2 fresh bay leaves

1 tablespoon chopped fresh rosemary, plus extra sprigs to garnish (optional)

1 tablespoon chopped fresh sage

sea salt and freshly ground black pepper

freshly grated Parmesan, to serve

fresh egg pasta

300 g plain white flour or Italian 00 flour

a pinch of salt

3 eggs

1½ tablespoons olive oil, plus a little extra

semolina flour or fine cornmeal, for dusting

a pasta machine

serves 4

Cut all the meat off the bones with a sharp knife. Cut the meat into small dice or put through a mincer or food processor. Heat the oil and butter in a sauté pan and add the chopped onion, carrot, celery and garlic. Stir well and cook gently for about 10 minutes until soft and beginning to brown. Add the pancetta and hare, stir well and cook for a couple of minutes until the meat is browned. Alternatively, cut the meat into joints, brown and cook with all the other ingredients, then lift out and cut the meat off the bone, then dice and return to the sauce. Season well with salt and pepper. Stir in the flour, then the wine and half the stock. Mix well, scraping any sediment lodged on the base of the pan. Add the herbs and bring to the boil. Turn down the heat, half cover and simmer gently for at least 2 hours, topping up with more stock as necessary, until the meat is very tender and the sauce thick, dark and reduced.

Meanwhile, to make the fresh egg pasta, sift the flour and salt onto a clean work surface and make a hollow in the centre with your fist. Beat the eggs and olive oil in a bowl, then pour into the hollow in the flour. Gradually mix the eggs into the flour with the fingers of one hand, and bring it together to form a dough. Knead the pasta until smooth, lightly massage with a hint of olive oil, put in a plastic bag and let rest for at least 30 minutes.

Cut the pasta in two and cover one of the pieces. Using a pasta machine, gradually roll out the other piece setting by setting, from the widest to the penultimate setting. Dust the pasta thoroughly with semolina flour then loosely roll up from the short ends towards the middle like a Swiss roll. Cut into 2.5 cm wide slices with one downwards cut each time with a sharp knife. Immediately unravel the slices to reveal the pasta ribbons, dust with more semolina and arrange in loose bundles on floured tea towels. To give the pappardelle fluted edges, use a fluted pastry wheel to cut wide ribbons from the rolled out pasta dough. Repeat with the remaining pasta dough.

Bring a large pan of salted water to the boil and drop in the pasta. Stir well, then boil for 1 minute, then drain. Toss with a little melted butter and arrange on a platter. Taste the sauce, season as necessary and remove the bay leaves. Liquidize to make it finer, if liked. Spoon on top of the pappardelle and garnish with rosemary sprigs, if liked. Serve immediately with Parmesan.

Malfatti means 'badly formed'. The less you handle these gnocchi, the lighter they are, so odd shapes don't matter. These are the lightest form of gnocchi, especially when made with snowy white, fresh ricotta sold in Italian delicatessens. Ricotta is made from whey left after making either cows' milk or sheep's milk cheeses. The ricotta that is sold in tubs in supermarkets is made from pasteurized whole milk.

spinach and ricotta gnocchi in lemon broth
malfatti in brodo

675 g fresh spinach or 300 g frozen spinach, thawed

25 g butter

1 shallot, finely chopped

finely grated zest of 2 unwaxed lemons

150 g fresh ricotta, sieved

50 g plain flour

2 egg yolks

75 g freshly grated Parmesan or pecorino cheese, plus extra to serve

freshly grated nutmeg

400 ml vegetable or chicken stock

sea salt and freshly ground black pepper

plain flour or semolina flour, for sprinkling

serves 4

If using fresh spinach, remove the stalks and wash the leaves in several changes of cold water. Drain well, then put in a large saucepan with just the water left clinging to the leaves. Cook until just wilted. Let cool slightly, then squeeze out most of the moisture. Chop roughly and set aside. If using frozen spinach, squeeze the moisture out of it and chop roughly.

Melt the butter in the saucepan and fry the shallot until golden. Stir in the spinach and the zest of 1 lemon and cook for a couple of minutes until coated and mixed with the butter and shallot. Tip into a large bowl. Beat in the ricotta, flour, egg yolks and Parmesan. When well-mixed, taste and season well with salt, pepper and nutmeg. Cover and chill in the refrigerator for a couple of hours or overnight, if possible, to firm up.

When you are ready to cook the gnocchi, put the stock in a large saucepan, add the remaining lemon zest and heat until boiling. Strain and keep warm.

Take teaspoonfuls of the gnocchi mixture and quickly roll into very small balls, but not too neatly. Alternatively, shape the gnocchi mixture into ovals using 2 teaspoons. Put them on a tray lined with a tea towel lightly sprinkled with flour. Bring a large saucepan of salted water to the boil. Gently drop in the gnocchi and cook for 2–3 minutes, they should be ready when they rise to the surface. Remove with a slotted spoon and transfer to warm serving bowls. Pour the hot stock over the gnocchi and serve immediately with extra Parmesan sprinkled over.

little potato gnocchi with sage butter
topini

The Italian word *topini* means 'little mice', and this is what they are affectionately known as in Tuscany. Only use white-fleshed floury potatoes for gnocchi. New potatoes will make them gluey and chewy. It takes a little practice to make gnocchi really light, as overworking makes them tough. Some expert gnocchi makers make them without any egg at all – do not try this at home!

600 g floury potatoes

200 g butter, melted

1 egg, beaten

200 g plain white flour, plus extra for dusting

2 tablespoons finely chopped fresh sage

sea salt and freshly ground black pepper

50 g finely grated Parmesan cheese

serves 4

Cook the potatoes in boiling water for 20–30 minutes until very tender, then drain well. Halve the potatoes and press through a potato ricer, or peel and press through a sieve into a bowl. While they are still warm, add 1 teaspoon salt, the beaten egg and the flour. Lightly mix together, then turn out onto a floured board. Knead lightly to yield a smooth, soft, slightly sticky dough. Roll the dough into long 'sausages', 1.5 cm in diameter. Cut into 2 cm pieces and shape into corks or pull each one down over the back of a fork to produce the traditional ridged outside and the hollow inside. Lay them on a lightly floured tea towel.

Bring a large pan of salted water to the boil. Cook the gnocchi in batches. Drop them into the boiling water and cook for 2–3 minutes or until they float to the surface. Remove with a slotted spoon immediately they rise and keep hot while cooking the remainder. Meanwhile, mix the butter and the sage in a small bowl, reheat, taste and season with salt and pepper. Pour over the sage butter, scatter with the Parmesan and serve immediately.

Often this is poured onto a serving dish and topped with a rich meat sauce, to be eaten straight from the dish. Sometimes the polenta is moulded into egg shapes with two spoons dipped in water, but I find it easier to let it set, then stamp out shapes with a biscuit cutter. It makes a nice change to use a non-meat sauce with this – dried porcini mushrooms add body to a rich tomato sauce.

baked polenta gnocchi
gnocchi di granoturco al forno

400 g polenta

1 recipe *Sugo di Funghi e Pomodori* (page 71)

100 g freshly grated Parmesan cheese

sea salt

serves 4

Bring 1½ litres of salted water to the boil, then slowly sprinkle in the polenta flour through your fingers whisking all the time to prevent lumps. Cook on a low heat for 45 minutes, stirring with a wooden spoon, and then turn out into a mound onto a wooden board and leave to cool and set.

Line a shallow dish with clingfilm and spoon the polenta into it, smoothing the surface, then allow to cool. When cold, turn out the polenta and remove the clingfilm. Cut into as many rounds as possible. Arrange a layer of the polenta off-cuts to cover the base of a buttered ovenproof dish. Cover with half the sauce and half the Parmesan. Cover with another layer of polenta, the remaining sauce and the remaining Parmesan. At this stage, the dish can be covered and refrigerated until needed. Bake in a preheated oven at 180°C (350°F) Gas 4 for 40 minutes until brown and bubbling.

Italian sausages are pure minced pork – nothing added except salt and pepper and maybe chilli or fennel seeds. They have a much better flavour and texture than ordinary sausages, so it's worth seeking out a good Italian delicatessen in your area. In Italy, you choose your cut of pork and the sausages are made in moments right in front of you, leaving you to choose your personal seasoning preference. Tuscans like their sausages flavoured with fennel seeds and plenty of black pepper. In fact, a Tuscan friend once gave me a jar of crushed wild fennel flowers (fennel pollen) which added an incredible flavour to this risotto.

fennel sausage risotto
risotto di salsicce al finocchio

about 1.5 litres hot chicken or vegetable stock

125 g butter

450 g fresh Italian fennel sausages, skins removed

1 onion, finely chopped

2 garlic cloves, finely chopped

150 ml Italian sieved tomatoes *(passata)*

1 tablespoon fresh thyme

1 tablespoon fennel seeds

500 g Italian risotto rice, preferably arborio or carnaroli

75 g freshly grated Parmesan cheese, plus extra to serve

sea salt and freshly ground black pepper

thyme sprigs, to garnish (optional)

serves 6

Put the stock in a saucepan on the stove and keep at a gentle simmer. Melt half the butter in a large, heavy-based saucepan then add the sausage. Cook over a medium heat for 3–4 minutes, squashing it with a spoon to break it up. Add the onion and garlic and cook gently for 10 minutes until the onion is soft and golden. Add the passata, fennel seeds and thyme and simmer for 5–10 minutes. Stir in the rice making sure it is heated through.

Begin to add the stock a large ladleful at a time, stirring gently until each ladleful is almost absorbed into the rice. The risotto should be kept at a bare simmer throughout cooking, so do not let the rice dry out – add more stock as necessary. Continue until the rice is tender and creamy, but the grains still firm. This should take between 15–20 minutes depending on the type of rice used – look at the manufacturer's instructions.

Taste and season well with salt and pepper and beat in the remaining butter and the Parmesan. Cover and rest for a couple of minutes to allow the risotto to relax and the cheese to melt. You may like to add a little more hot stock just before you serve to loosen it, but don't let the risotto hang around too long or the rice will turn mushy. Serve in warm bowls, sprinkled with Parmesan and garnished with thyme sprigs, if liked.

sauces

fiery red pepper sauce
salsa piccante di peperoni

A rustic sauce for pasta inspired by the spicy pepper dishes made in Elba, the island just off the coast of southern Tuscany. Fresh hot peppers or long chillies (*peperoncini*) are used a lot there, whether red or green. Use rubber gloves when preparing chillies.

6 sweet red peppers, halved and deseeded
2 large red chillies, halved and deseeded
4 tablespoons extra virgin olive oil
2 garlic cloves, finely chopped
4 ripe tomatoes, chopped
2 tablespoons chopped fresh basil
sea salt and freshly ground black pepper

serves 4

Cut the peppers into medium dice and finely chop the chillies. Heat the olive oil in a frying pan and add the garlic. Cook for 1 minute until golden but not brown. Stir in the peppers and chillies and cook slowly for about 20 minutes until really soft.

Add the tomatoes, season with salt and pepper, then half cover and simmer gently for 20 minutes until well-reduced, soft and thick. You may have to add a little water to keep the sauce from sticking. Just before serving, stir in the basil and toss with your chosen cooked pasta.

mushroom and tomato sauce
sugo di funghi e pomodori

If you are lucky enough to have an abundant supply of fresh wild porcini mushrooms, this is the sauce to make. Tuscans are crazy for porcini and spend hours of their spare time foraging on the bosky hillsides – it is seen as their birthright. The herb nepitella (botanical name, *Nepeta nepetella*) grows wild all over Tuscany and is frequently added to your porcini purchase at the market. It tastes a little like a mixture of mint, thyme and oregano. However, you can conjure up the same pungent flavour by using a mixture of cultivated open-cup mushrooms mixed with a handful of soaked dried porcini and a similar mixture of dried herbs. This is delicious served with soft polenta, gnocchi or even pappardelle.

300 g fresh porcini or large open-cup cultivated mushrooms
30 g dried porcini mushrooms, soaked for 30 minutes in warm water
75 ml extra virgin olive oil
3 garlic cloves, finely chopped
400 g fresh ripe tomatoes or 400 g canned chopped tomatoes
1 teaspoon mixed dried mint, oregano and thyme
sea salt and freshly ground black pepper

serves 4

Clean the wild mushrooms by brushing them lightly with a pastry brush to remove any grit or dried leaves. Trim the bases of the stems. Wipe the cultivated mushrooms but do not peel or wash. Pull the caps from the stalks and chop them all into small dice.

Heat the olive oil in a saucepan and add the mushrooms and garlic. Toss over a fairly high heat for 2–3 minutes. Add the tomatoes then the herbs, salt and pepper. Bring to the boil then simmer and half covered for 20 minutes or until the oil starts to separate on the surface and the sauce is reduced. Taste and check the seasoning.

rich tuscan meat sauce
sugo toscano di carne

A classic meat sauce is always started off with a *battuto* (a very finely chopped mixture) of celery, onion and carrot, and sometimes garlic. When this vegetable mixture is fried it becomes a *soffritto*. It is important not to brown the meat too much – it should brown just enough to turn from raw to cooked, then it will remain soft. Cook the sauce very slowly, between 1–3 hours, as the longer it simmers, the better it will taste. You can make a big batch in a large covered casserole and simmer it in the oven at 150°C (300°F) Gas 2 for 3 hours and freeze what you don't use. This sauce can be served with *Pici* (page 56) or polenta.

25–50 g dried porcini mushrooms
2 tablespoons extra virgin olive oil
50 g butter
1 small onion, finely chopped
1 small carrot, finely chopped
1 stick of celery, finely chopped
300 g lean beef, veal or pork mince
50 g pancetta with plenty of fat, minced or finely chopped
4 tablespoons dry red wine
400 g Italian sieved tomatoes (*passata*) or puréed chopped tomatoes
1 tablespoon tomato purée
500 ml meat stock
1 bay leaf
115 g plump fresh chicken livers, trimmed and very finely chopped
sea salt and freshly ground black pepper

serves 4–6

Cover the mushrooms in warm water and leave to soak. Meanwhile, melt the butter in the oil over a medium heat in a heavy casserole and add the onion, carrot and celery. Cook for 5–10 minutes until golden, but not brown. Add the meat and pancetta and brown very lightly, breaking up any large lumps. Add the wine, turn up the heat and boil until evaporated. Reduce the heat, then add the passata and the tomato purée, mix well then add the stock, bay leaf, salt and pepper. Bring to the boil, stir well, then half cover and simmer for about 2 hours, topping up with a little water to prevent it drying out.

After 1½ hours, drain the mushrooms, reserving the liquid, chop finely and add to the sauce with the chicken livers. Stir well, add a splash of reserved mushroom water, then simmer for a further 30 minutes or until the butter and oil begins to separate on the surface. It should be rich and thick. Season well.

duck sauce from arezzo
sugo aretino

Duck is very popular in this region. The commercially available species is the *muschiata* or *muta* (Muscovy duck) and the smaller wild duck are *germano reale* (mallard) and *fischioine* (widgeon). Game is highly prized and makes the centrepiece of a winter meal. This sauce can be served with pasta, rice or polenta and is sometimes liquidized to make it finer.

3 tablespoons olive oil
1 whole duck or 1 kg of duck joints, including legs and breast
1 onion, finely diced
1 carrot, finely diced
1 stick of celery, finely diced
2 garlic cloves, chopped
75 g unsmoked pancetta, finely diced
300 ml dry white wine
400 g can chopped tomatoes
300 ml game or good-quality chicken stock
30 g dried porcini mushrooms, soaked in warm water for 30 minutes
2 fresh bay leaves
2 tablespoons chopped fresh sage
sea salt and freshly ground black pepper

serves 4

Heat the olive oil in a sauté pan and fry the duck pieces until golden. Add the onion, carrot, celery, garlic and pancetta. Stir well and cook gently for about 10 minutes until soft and beginning to brown. Pour in the wine, boil until evaporated, then add the tomatoes and stock, mixing well and scraping away any sediment lodged on the base of the pan. Drain the mushrooms and add to the pan with the herbs, then bring to the boil. Turn down the heat, half cover and simmer gently for at least 2 hours, topping up with a little water as necessary, until the meat is very tender.

Take the pan off the heat. Lift out the duck pieces, remove the skin and discard, then pull the meat off the bones and either chop it up or pull into fine shreds. Skim the fat off the surface of the sauce and stir in the duck meat. Taste the sauce, season as necessary and reheat. Remove the bay leaves before serving.

walnut and caper pesto
pesto alle noci e capperi

In late Tuscan summer we eat lunch in the shade of a huge walnut tree and literally have walnuts dropping onto the table, which is handy for the last course of the meal. We gathered these small creamy nuts and made this sauce to have with our own spinach tagliatelle. It also goes wonderfully with *Topini* (page 64) or potato gnocchi. You can freeze this pesto in ice-cube trays, then pop them out into plastic bags.

2 garlic cloves, peeled

85 g walnut halves, fresh if possible

2 tablespoons capers in salt, rinsed

50 g fresh parsley leaves

200 ml extra virgin olive oil, plus extra for preserving

50 g unsalted butter, softened

4 tablespoons freshly grated pecorino cheese

sea salt and freshly ground black pepper

serves 4–6

Put the garlic, walnuts, capers and a little salt in a pestle and mortar, then pound until broken up. Add the parsley, a few leaves at a time, pounding and mixing to a paste. Gradually beat in the olive oil until creamy and thick. Beat in the butter, season with pepper, then beat in the pecorino. Alternatively, process the ingredients in a food processor until smooth.

Store in a jar, with a layer of olive oil on top to exclude the air, in the refrigerator until needed. Level the surface each time you use it, and re-cover the pesto with olive oil.

tuscan basil, parsley and anchovy pesto
pesto toscano

A beautiful piquant pesto made without any cheese. It is important to weigh the basil and parsley leaves to achieve the correct result. Tuscan sauces usually have a rustic appearance, as it was traditional for cooks to use a mezzaluna for chopping instead of a pestle and mortar. It is delicious with fish, chicken and meat dishes rather than with pasta. This makes quite a loose sauce, keeps well in the refrigerator but it doesn't freeze well.

1 garlic clove, peeled

3 tablespoons pine nuts

2 anchovy fillets in oil, rinsed

30 g basil leaves

30 g flat leaf parsley leaves

1 tablespoon red wine vinegar

150 ml extra virgin olive oil, plus extra for preserving

sea salt and freshly ground black pepper

serves 6

Put the garlic, pine nuts and anchovies and a little salt in a pestle and mortar and pound until broken up. Add the basil and parsley leaves a few at a time, pounding and mixing to a rough paste. Stir in the vinegar, then gradually stir in the olive oil until the mixture is thick and well blended. Taste and season with salt and pepper. Alternatively, process the ingredients in a food processor until roughly blended.

Store in a jar, with a layer of olive oil on top to exclude the air, in the refrigerator until needed. Level the surface each time you use it and re-cover the pesto with olive oil.

tarragon pesto
salsa di dragoncello

When I was studying in Florence many years ago, *dragoncello* was one of the first Italian words I learnt. The owner of the little shop I used to buy my vegetables from made me repeat the Italian names of everything I bought, before I left the shop. It is one of my favourite Italian words as it sounds magical! This is a wonderfully powerful sauce to serve in small quantities with meat or poultry – the Tuscan equivalent of British mint sauce. The ingredients are usually finely hand-chopped, as is usual in these parts, but it really is easier made in a food processor.

6 large sprigs fresh tarragon
2 garlic cloves, chopped
50 g fresh white breadcrumbs
2 teaspoons red wine vinegar
about 150 ml extra virgin olive oil
sea salt and freshly ground black pepper

serves 4–6

Pull the tarragon leaves off the stalks, wash and pat dry. Put the leaves in a food processor with the garlic and breadcrumbs and process in short bursts until finely chopped. Sprinkle with the vinegar and add a little salt and pepper. With the machine running, slowly add the olive oil until the sauce is amalgamated and pourable.

Store in a jar, for up to 1 week in the refrigerator, covered with a layer of olive oil.

fresh garlic sauce
agliata

This sauce is quite fabulous made with the first garlic of the season, sometimes known as wet garlic, as it has a milder flavour than end-of-season garlic. If using older garlic, remember to halve the cloves and remove any green shoots inside as they can taste bitter. As with all simple things, good ingredients are essential, so do use really good olive oil. It is usually served with cooked meats, poultry or fish.

4 garlic cloves, chopped
50 g fresh white breadcrumbs
about 2 teaspoons white wine vinegar
200 ml extra virgin olive oil, plus extra for preserving
sea salt and freshly ground black pepper

serves 4

Put the garlic in a food processor with the breadcrumbs and process in short bursts until finely chopped. Sprinkle with the vinegar and add a little salt and pepper. With the machine running, slowly add the olive oil until the sauce is creamy and smooth. Taste and season, adding extra vinegar if necessary.

Store in a jar, for up to 1 week in the refrigerator, covered with a layer of olive oil.

anchovy and garlic sauce
acciugata

Salted anchovies have much more flavour than anchovies in oil – they add a savoury saltiness to all types of bland dishes and are generally used in small quantities as a seasoning, like salt and pepper. This is one of the few Tuscan sauces to serve with pasta, but it is even nicer stirred into warm white beans.

4 whole anchovies, preserved in salt
1 garlic clove
150 ml extra virgin olive oil

serves 4

Clean the anchovies, then open up the body cavity and loosen the backbone. Lift out the backbone then rinse the fillets in cold water. Pat dry then chop finely. Crack the garlic clove with the end of a rolling pin, but it must remain whole.

Heat the olive oil in a small saucepan and add the garlic. Cook for 1–2 minutes over a gentle heat until golden, but not brown. Lift it out then stir in the anchovies. Mix well until they dissolve into the sauce.

salsa verde
green herb sauce

This beautiful green sauce takes its colour from a generous mixture of green herbs. Often it is made predominantly with parsley and is served with the famous dish of boiled meats known as *bollito misto*. Like many Tuscans, I prefer a punchier, herby flavour and add mint and basil to the sauce. I love the fresh acidity of lemon juice, which is particularly good when serving with fish, but you can add vinegar to taste instead, which I find is better with meat. The sauce can be liquidized for a smoother, more sophisticated sauce – but I like a rougher look.

1 teaspoon sea salt
2 garlic cloves, finely chopped
4 anchovy fillets in oil, rinsed and finely chopped
3 tablespoons chopped fresh parsley
3 tablespoons chopped fresh mint
3 tablespoons chopped fresh basil
2 tablespoons salted capers, rinsed and chopped
150 ml extra virgin olive oil, plus extra for preserving
2 tablespoons freshly squeezed lemon juice, or to taste
freshly ground black pepper

serves 4–6

Pound 1 teaspoon of salt with the garlic in a pestle and mortar until creamy – the salt helps to break down the garlic. Stir in the anchovies, parsley, mint, basil, capers, olive oil and lemon juice and season with black pepper. Transfer to a jar and pour a layer of olive oil on top to exclude the air. This will keep up to a week in the refrigerator.

secondi

fish and seafood
meat, poultry and game

A particularly Tuscan way of cooking almost any type of fish with spinach, tomatoes and the familiar trinity of carrot, onion and celery with herbs. The fish keeps beautifully moist as it is literally steamed on top of the vegetables. It is always best to cook fish on the bone for a better flavour, but chunks of fish or even fillets are good, but will take less time to cook. Salt cod is delicious cooked this way.

fish cooked on a bed of spinach or swiss chard and tomatoes
pesce allo inzimino

75 ml extra virgin olive oil

1 small carrot, finely diced

1 small onion, finely diced

1 celery stick, finely diced

2 garlic cloves, chopped

100 ml dry white wine

300 ml Italian sieved tomatoes *(passata)*

750 g Swiss chard or fresh leaf spinach

4 whole white fish, about 250 g each, cleaned and scaled, or 750 g fish fillets or cubes

sea salt and freshly ground black pepper

2 tablespoons chopped fresh parsley, to serve

serves 4

Heat the oil in a wide saucepan and add the carrot, onion, celery and garlic. Cook for 10 minutes until golden, then add the wine and boil until evaporated. Pour in the passata and bring to the boil. Season with salt and pepper and simmer gently for 10 minutes.

Meanwhile, strip the green leaf from the white central stems of the chard. Roughly chop the leaves and slice the stems, rinse well and drain. If using spinach, strip the leaves off the stems, discard the stems and roughly chop the leaves. Stir the chard or spinach into the sauce and bring to the boil. Lay the whole fish or fish fillets on top, or push in the fish chunks. Cover, reduce the heat and cook at a bare simmer for 10–15 minutes if using fish fillets or chunks, or 20 minutes if using whole fish. Remove the lid and season well with black pepper and a little salt. Sprinkle with parsley and serve with lots of bread.

sardines with currants and pine nuts
sarde in dolceforte

The mixture of sweet and savoury with fish is popular all over Italy – every region has its own version. The method of frying fish then marinating in reduced vinegar and raisins or currants was meant to preserve the fish for a short period of time before refrigeration was available. This will work with all oily fish – even salmon.

16 fresh sardines, about 600 g

4 tablespoons extra virgin olive oil

1 large onion, thinly sliced

3 tablespoons raisins

3 tablespoons pine nuts

200 ml white wine vinegar

plain flour, for coating

sea salt and freshly ground black pepper

3 tablespoons chopped fresh parsley,
to serve

serves 4

Scale the sardines, cut off the heads and slit open the bellies. Remove the guts under running water. Slide your thumb along the backbone to release the flesh along its length. Take hold of the backbone at the head end and lift it out. The fish should now be open like a book. Rinse and pat dry. Dip the sardines in flour seasoned with salt and pepper and shake off the excess.

Heat 2 tablespoons olive oil in a large frying pan and fry the sardines on both sides until golden and cooked through. Lift out and put onto a platter or shallow serving dish. Add the remaining olive oil, onion, raisins, pine nuts and vinegar to the pan and bring to the boil. Boil fast until evaporated by half. Pour over the sardines, cool, cover and chill. Serve the next day at room temperature sprinkled with the parsley.

salt cod fritters with a polenta crust
polpette di baccalà e polenta

100 g fine polenta

500 g pre-soaked salt cod (page 59)

3 eggs

2 tablespoons extra virgin olive oil, plus extra to serve

2 tablespoons chopped fresh parsley

plain flour, for coating

vegetable oil, for deep-frying

sea salt and freshly ground black pepper

lemon wedges, to serve

a deep-fryer

serves 4

Salt cod is often cooked and served on a bed of soft polenta, but I prefer incorporating the polenta to cut the saltiness of the cod, then using it as a crumb coating instead of breadcrumbs. Capers in vinegar are a good addition, and these are particularly good with a big blob of homemade mayonnaise and a salad.

Sprinkle 4 tablespoons polenta into a small bowl and add 3 tablespoons boiling water. Mix well with a fork, cover and leave to swell for 10 minutes. Meanwhile, rinse the salt cod, remove any skin and check for any bones. Cut into chunks and place in a food processor. Add the soaked polenta, 2 of the eggs, the olive oil, parsley and some black pepper. Process in short bursts until it is nicely minced and beginning to form a ball. Tip out and, using dampened hands, form into 12–16 smooth croquettes, then coat with flour. Beat the remaining egg and use to coat the croquettes. Finally roll them in the remaining polenta and set on a tray covered with clingfilm. Cover and chill for 30 minutes.

Heat the oil in a deep-fryer to 180°C (350°F) – a piece of stale bread dropped in should turn golden in a few seconds. Fry the croquettes in batches for 4–5 minutes until deep golden. Lift out and drain on kitchen paper before serving with lemon wedges and olive oil.

red mullet with garlic and tomato sauce
triglie alla livornese

6 tablespoons extra virgin olive oil

1 stick of celery, finely chopped

3 garlic cloves, chopped

4 tablespoons chopped fresh parsley

600 g ripe red tomatoes, peeled
and chopped

a pinch of dried chilli flakes

4 large red mullet or 8 small ones, cleaned
and scaled

plain flour, for coating

sea salt and freshly ground black pepper

serves 4

This is traditionally cooked on the coastline around Livorno and almost always with red mullet. However, it is delicious with cod, haddock, pollock, John Dory, in fact any white fish. Italians tend to eat whole fish – they don't mind the occasional bone and are taught how to tackle a whole fish from birth. This is traditionally served with *Fagioli all'Uccelletto* (page 121) or fresh peas.

Heat 4 tablespoons olive oil and add the celery, garlic and half the parsley. Cook for a few minutes then add the chopped tomatoes, chilli, salt and pepper. Bring to the boil then simmer for 10 minutes.

Meanwhile, dip the fish in flour and shake off the excess. Heat the remaining oil in a frying pan and fry the fish for a few minutes on both sides until golden. Pour in the tomato sauce and bring to the boil. Simmer for a couple more minutes until the fish is cooked through and will flake easily. Serve at once, sprinkled with the remaining parsley.

tuna steaks baked with rosemary
tonno al cartoccio al rosmarino

Tuna is a very filling and rich fish. Although one never thinks of cooking it with rosemary, it is a marriage made in heaven. Especially when flavoured with good olive oil and some capers to cut the richness.

Coat the tuna steaks with the rosemary. Transfer each steak onto a big square of baking parchment or kitchen foil. Scatter the capers on top then pour the wine over. Season well with salt and pepper, then drizzle with olive oil. Loosely but securely twist or close the paper or foil around the tuna – it should be loose enough to fill with steam as it cooks, but secure enough not to let the juices escape during the cooking. Bake in a preheated oven at 180°C (350°F) Gas 4 for 15 minutes. Serve each packet on a hot plate for each diner to open for themselves, with lemon wedges and garnished with rosemary sprigs, if liked.

4 x 150 g tuna steaks

2 tablespoons chopped fresh rosemary, plus extra sprigs to garnish (optional)

1 tablespoon salted capers, rinsed and dried and chopped

4 tablespoons dry white wine

4 tablespoons extra virgin olive oil

sea salt and freshly ground black pepper

lemon wedges, to serve

serves 4

Mussels are called *muscoli* in local dialect as opposed to Italian *cozze*. The contrast of the golden crunchy breadcrumbs, the spicy salami and the soft mussel meat is fantastic and although this seems a lot of work, it is well worth it! It is interesting to know that the bright orange-fleshed mussels are female and the whitish ones are male – there is nothing wrong with them, they just don't look so appetizing. This is my adaptation of one of the most popular dishes eaten in coastal areas. I have used spicy salami where others might use fresh pork sausage.

mussels baked under crispy breadcrumbs
muscoli ripieni

1.5 kg fresh mussels, cleaned

150 ml white wine

2 garlic cloves, peeled and lightly crushed

a pinch of dried chilli flakes

1 onion, very finely chopped

3 tablespoons olive oil, plus extra for drizzling

150 g stale, but not dried, breadcrumbs

4 tablespoons finely chopped parsley

85 g spicy salami, finely diced

freshly squeezed juice of 1 lemon

sea salt and freshly ground black pepper

serves 4 as a starter

Scrub and debeard the mussels. Tap all the mussels against the work surface. Discard any that don't close – they are dead – and also any with damaged shells. Keep in a bowl of cold water until ready to cook.

Put the mussels in a large pan with the wine, garlic, and chilli flakes, cover and cook over a high heat for about 4–5 minutes until they just start to open. Discard any that do not open. Strain through a large sieve and reserve the juices. When the mussels have cooled, twist off and discard all the empty shells and arrange the mussels in a single layer in a large baking dish or individual baking dishes set on a baking tray.

Fry the onion in olive oil for about 5 minutes until soft. Reduce the heat and add the breadcrumbs and parsley and stir so that all the breadcrumbs absorb the oil, and cook for a further 5 minutes to brown slightly. Stir in the salami. Pile this mix over each mussel to cover, drizzle with olive oil and lemon juice, season with black pepper and bake in a preheated oven at 220°C (425°F) Gas 7 for 5 minutes.

Reheat the reserved strained mussel liquid and pour around the mussels before serving. Good bread is an essential accompaniment here!

squid sautéd with potatoes and chilli
seppie con patate e peperoncino

800 g fresh whole squid

150 ml extra virgin olive oil

4 garlic cloves, chopped

150 ml dry white wine

½–1 teaspoon dried chilli flakes

750 g yellow-fleshed potatoes, peeled and cut into chunks, or small new potatoes, halved

3 tablespoons chopped fresh parsley

sea salt and freshly ground black pepper

lemon wedges, to serve

serves 4

There's something about the sweetness of squid and the fire of chilli that marries very well. Tuscans are particularly fond of small amounts of chilli as they find it good for the digestion. This dish can be made with ready-cleaned squid, in which case you will need about 150 g per person. This is one of the best ways of cooking squid as the long cooking ensures that it is tender.

To clean the squid, pull the head from the body. Remove the 'plastic quill' from the inside of the squid tube. Rinse the tubes and slice into rings. Trim the tentacles from the head by holding the head just below the eyes and cutting the tentacles away. Pop out the 'beak' from the tentacles. Rinse, discarding the head and entrails.

Heat the oil in a casserole and add the garlic, cook for about 1 minute, then add the squid and stir-fry for about 1 minute. Pour in the wine and add the chilli flakes. Bring to the boil then cover and simmer very gently for 30 minutes – you may have to top up the liquid at least once to prevent it sticking. Stir in the potatoes with 75 ml water, season with salt and pepper, cover and cook very gently for another 25 minutes. Stir well, then sprinkle with parsley and serve immediately with lemon wedges.

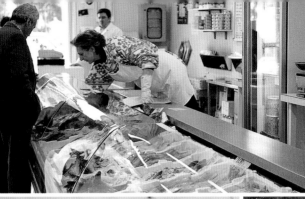
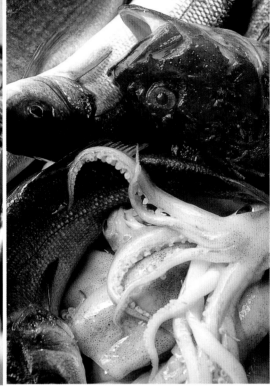
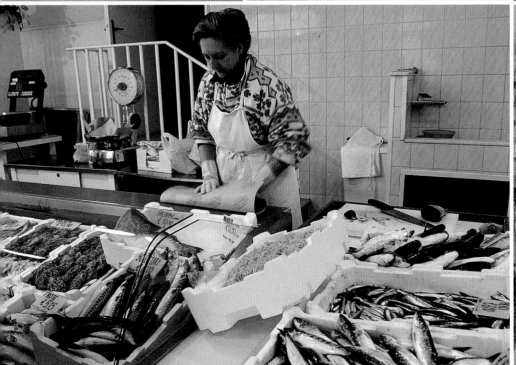

I use medium-sized, fresh raw unpeeled prawns *(gamberi)*, but remove the heads before cooking, although Italians prefer them in the sauce so that they can pull of the heads and suck out the juices! The heads can be used to make a wonderful stock to add to the sauce. This dish can also be made with mixed seafood such as mussels, clams and squid – whatever is around.

prawns in tomato sauce with chickpea pasta
gamberi

3 garlic cloves, finely chopped

3 tablespoons extra virgin olive oil, plus extra to serve

1 fresh hot red chilli, deseeded and finely chopped or a large pinch of chilli powder (optional)

500 g ripe tomatoes, peeled and chopped, or cherry tomatoes, halved

250 ml dry white wine

1–2 teaspoons sugar, to taste

500 g shelled raw tiger prawns

4 tablespoons finely chopped flat leaf parsley, plus extra to garnish

sea salt and freshly ground black pepper

chickpea pasta

200 g chickpea flour or gram flour

200 g plain white flour or Italian 00 flour

a pinch of salt

4 eggs

2 tablespoons olive oil, plus a little extra

semolina flour or fine cornmeal, for dusting

serves 4

a pasta machine

To make the chickpea pasta, sift the flours and salt onto a clean work surface and make a hollow in the centre with your fist. Put the eggs and olive oil in a bowl, beat well, then pour into the hollow in the flour. Gradually mix the eggs into the flour with the fingers of one hand, and bring it together to form a dough. Knead the pasta until smooth, lightly massage with a hint of olive oil, put in a plastic bag and let rest for at least 30 minutes.

Cut the pasta in two and cover one of the pieces. Using a pasta machine, gradually roll out the other piece, setting by setting starting at the widest, to the penultimate setting. Dust the pasta thoroughly with semolina flour then loosely roll up from the short ends towards the middle like a Swiss roll. Cut into 1 cm wide slices with one sharp downwards cut each time with a sharp knife. Immediately unravel the slices to reveal the tagliatelle, dust with more semolina flour and arrange in loose bundles on floured tea towels. Repeat with the other piece of pasta.

Fry the garlic in the oil until it just begins to colour. Add the chilli and tomatoes, and cook for 5 minutes. Add the wine and stock, if using (see above). Season to taste with salt and pepper, add the sugar, then simmer for 10 minutes to reduce by half.

Add the prawns and simmer for 3 minutes, then stir in the parsley. Cook the pasta in plenty of boiling water for 1 minute, then drain toss with olive oil and serve with the sauce poured over, sprinkled with chopped parsley.

white cattle of the Val de Chiana

My choice for a 'last request meal' would be a perfectly grilled steak and a bottle of ridiculously good red wine. To qualify this further, it would have to be an aged *Bistecca alla Fiorentina* (page 96) cooked over oak embers by my friend and cooking mentor, Marcella Libertini. It would be simply dressed with extra virgin olive oil, salt and pepper and accompanied by a bottle of Fattoria di Felsina's Fontalloro. I would want nothing else with it – not even a salad – and it would be sublime!

In Tuscany, size certainly matters when it comes to beef and steaks, and the ancient Chianina, or Maremmana Chianino, breed of beef cattle from the Val de Chiana, south of Arezzo, are, to put it mildly, enormous. They are also beautiful. Calves are born a fawn colour and turn white between 1 and 9 months. Mature cattle are a creamy white colour with a black tongue and nose and inky black eyes that look as if they have enjoyed the services of a top make-up artist in applying perfect black eyeliner and mascara. The horns are short and turn from black, when young, to white, when around 2 years old. These magnificent beasts stand very tall and long. Mature bulls stand 180 cm (6 feet) at the withers. The sheer size of the reproductive organs alone would make anyone blush!

These exquisite, hardy animals have been known in Italy since Etruscan times. The Romans used them as sacrifices in religious festivals and as beasts of burden in triumphs. Chianina cattle are perfect for cross-breeding and have been exported throughout the world, particularly to hotter countries where other breeds would not be able to survive.

Apart from their beauty and size, Chianinas are delicious to eat. They are late-maturing, and are therefore suitable for production of yearling and older beef. On my travels around Italy, I have found the terms used for different types of beef confusing, so here's a quick guide. This doesn't refer to the cuts, as the names for the same cuts vary enormously region to region, but to the variations on the word 'beef'. You often see the word *bue* (which means ox, strictly speaking) or *manzo* (beef) used in the same context. They both refer to a castrated male of the same breed, but term *bue* describes a younger animal from 1½ to 4 years old, while *manzo* is used for an older animal.

Vitellone (young beef) refers to an animal slaughtered between 14 and 16 months old. Its meat is firmer than veal and more tender than beef. *Torello* (young bull) refers to an uncastrated male, raised for slaughter. These young bulls are usually slaughtered at 2 years, at which time the meat is lean, tender and full of flavour. The meat is a good red colour with a perfect amount of fine marbling

throughout. They are fed a diet of corn, beans and barley. This pure-quality animal is not one that lends itself to intensive farming as it takes too long to reach maturity.

Given its impressive stature, its not surprising that a steak cut from this animal is super size. A true Florentine steak comes from a *vitellone* of the Chianina breed and it is cut from the loin, giving a T-bone steak that includes the fillet and the sirloin. It is typically hung for around 5 days and must be at least 3 cm thick. It must be seared very quickly (about 3 minutes on each side) about 10 cm above glowing wood embers, and should be seasoned only when seared (page 96). The secret to a tender, juicy steak is to cook it rare to medium rare. It should be simply dressed with the best-quality extra virgin olive oil, salt and pepper, and it is traditionally served sliced on wooden platters. You can buy a very simple iron contraption in Tuscany specifically designed for grilling large pieces of meat, which turns the meat over by means of a handle that you operate. It is worth investing in if you love this type of cooking and have some means of transporting it back home. I can't wait to return to Tuscany and buy one, but then again, my kitchen doesn't have a traditional brick hearth.

Another ancient breed of cattle in Tuscany is the Maremmana, who live in small herds on the drained marshland of the Maremma. This animal looks as if it has stepped out of an Egyptian tomb painting. It is large and muscular, light to dark grey in colour, with long slender black-tipped horns, which half-moon-shaped in bulls and lyre-shaped in cows. The horns of young animals are slate-grey. Calves are golden-coloured when born and gradually turn grey at around 3 months. Like the Chianina, they have black muzzles, tail and hoofs, but not the Cleopatra eyes!

The Maremmana is descended from the ancient breed *Bos taurus macroceros*, a longhorn cow originating from the Eurasian steppes, which can be traced back to the Etruscan era. These beautiful beasts were used for pulling carts and ploughs, and were later discovered to produce very good beef. Many years ago, they used to gather in enormous herds, running wild in the marshy, malaria-ridden Maremma in Tuscany and Latium. However, since the marshes were drained and machines took over from cattle, their numbers have decreased radically. Only now are they being recognized as good breeding stock and are used for cross-breeding all over Europe.

These cattle are perfectly suited to the harsh environment of the coastal marshland and populate areas that had previously been off-limits to other breeds. They live outside all year round and move from pastureland to marshlands to woods and scrub area, foraging off the land as much as possible. The herds are tended by Italian cowboys on horseback known as *butteri*.

Clockwise from top left: certified Chianina beef farm sign; Chianina cow; mature Chianina bull; Chianina cattle herd; Chianina calves.

barbecued steak
bistecca alla fiorentina

In Florence, size certainly matters – the size of your steak that is! The steaks are cut from young Chianina beef cattle that grow to an enormous size. The steaks are traditionally cooked against the mounded embers of a wood fire, the fat from the edge running over the surface of the meat to baste it. It should neither cook too quickly nor too slowly and must sear on the outside and remain pink and juicy inside. No oil is used to lubricate it and it is seasoned just before cooking. Quite an art, and best done on a barbecue.

2 large T-bone steaks, at least 750 g each or 2.5 cm thick
sea salt and freshly ground black pepper

a hinged double grill

serves 4

Light the barbecue and place the hinged grill on top to heat up. When the coals are no longer flaming and are covered with a grey ash, carefully open the grill, lay the steaks inside, then close. Cook for 3 minutes, season with salt and pepper, then turn them over and cook the other side for 3 minutes. Continue turning the steaks every 3 minutes until they are cooked medium or medium-rare and have a good colour on the outside – about 15 minutes in total, depending on the thickness. Let the steaks rest in a warm place for 10 minutes. Serve 1 steak between 2 people.

Stracotto means 'overcooked'. It is a very old recipe and was invented to make use of the tougher cuts of meat taken from an old and hard-working animal that needed long slow cooking, the prefix *stra* in Italian meaning 'too much'. Nowadays, it is usually made with *vitellone* (page 95). The Italian cuts of meat suitable for this, depending on the area, are: *la noce*, *il cimalino*, and *lo scanello*. This stew takes on the colour of the particular wine used.

beef stewed with tomato and mushrooms
stracotto alla fiorentina

1.2 kg beef silverside or topside, trimmed and tied

50 ml extra virgin olive oil

2 white onions, diced

2 stalks of celery, diced

2 carrots, diced

2 garlic cloves, chopped

250 g dried porcini mushrooms

2 bay leaves

4 sprigs of fresh thyme

4 leaves of fresh sage

300 ml dry red wine

1 litre meat stock

sea salt and freshly ground black pepper

thick slices of country bread, to serve

serves 6

Season the beef with salt and pepper. Heat the oil in the base of an oval casserole. Brown the meat well on all sides and transfer to a plate. Add the onions, celery, carrots, garlic, dried mushrooms and herbs. Cook these gently for about 15 minutes, stirring constantly so that they start to caramelize. Add the wine, then boil until evaporated. Pour in the stock, mix well then return the meat to the pan. Bring to the boil, then cover with dampened greaseproof paper and a lid.

Cook in a preheated oven at 180°C (350°F) Gas 4 for 3 hours, after which the meat should be beautifully tender. A knife inserted should meet no resistance. Lift out the meat and carve into slices. Liquidize the sauce, reheat, taste and check the seasoning. Serve the meat covered liberally in the sauce with plenty of bread for mopping up.

Redolent of early morning markets where *porchetta* (whole pigs stuffed and roasted overnight in wood-fired ovens) is sold sliced and crammed into huge buns as a morning snack, this dish recreates all those tastes and smells in your oven at home. Use as much rosemary as you can so the sweet pork flesh will be suffused with its pungent aroma. Tuscans cook this on the bone and slice into thick 'chops' when cooked – I think this is a more elegant way to cook it.

pork loin roasted with rosemary and garlic
arista alla fiorentina

1.75 kg loin of pork on the bone
4 large garlic cloves
4 tablespoons chopped fresh rosemary
a bunch of rosemary sprigs
300 ml dry white wine
extra virgin olive oil, for rubbing and frying
sea salt and freshly ground black pepper

serves 6

Ask the butcher to bone the loin, but to give you the bones. Also ask him to remove the skin and score it to make the crackling. Turn the loin fat side down. Make deep slits all over the meat, especially in the thick part. Make a paste of the garlic, chopped rosemary, at least 1 teaspoon of salt and pepper (more will give a truly authentic Tuscan flavour) in a food processor. Push this paste into all the slits in the meat and spread the remainder over the surface of the meat. Roll up and tie with fine string, incorporating some long sprigs of rosemary along its length. Weigh the meat and calculate the cooking time, allowing 25 minutes for every 500 g. At this stage you can wrap it and leave it in the refrigerator for several hours to deepen the flavour.

When ready to cook, heat 2 tablespoons olive oil in a frying pan, unwrap the pork and brown all over. Set in a roasting tin and pour the wine over the pork. Tuck in the remaining rosemary sprigs. Place the bones in another roasting pan convex side up. Rub the pork skin with a little oil and salt. Drape the skin over the pork bones. Place the pan of crackling on the top shelf of a preheated oven, and the pork on the bottom to middle shelf. Roast at 230°C (450°F) Gas 8 for 20 minutes then reduce the heat to 200°C (400°F) Gas 6, and roast for the remaining calculated time, basting the pork loin every 20 minutes.

When cooked, rest the pork in a warm place for 15 minutes before carving into thick slices. Serve with shards of crunchy crackling and the pan juices – there is no better gravy!

Here's another one that screams out to be barbecued. Tuscans love plainly grilled meat, and tend to add only their favourite herbs and good olive oil. This lamb is usually marinated then cooked on a spit, but I think it is easier to ask the butcher to butterfly the lamb (remove the bones and open it out flat). Doing this allows the marinade to penetrate the meat and, because the meat is now all one thickness, it will cook quickly and evenly.

marinated roast leg of lamb with garlic, rosemary and sage
agnello al rosmarino

2 kg leg of lamb

4 garlic cloves, crushed

3 tablespoons chopped rosemary

2 tablespoons chopped sage

3 tablespoons red wine vinegar

1 tablespoon balsamic vinegar

200 ml extra virgin olive oil

sea salt and freshly ground black pepper

serves 6–8

To bone the leg of lamb yourself, find the place where the longest bone running down the length of the leg appears to run quite close to the skin. Using a small sharp knife, slit through the thin surface along that bone and carefully peel the meat back from either side. Work round the bones at the thick end to release the meat, so that it opens up like a book and you can lift them out. Open out the meat, skin-side down – it should vaguely resemble the wings of a butterfly. Trim out any excess fat and score the meat where necessary to make it all the same thickness. Make deep slits all over the meat.

Mix the garlic and herbs with the vinegar and olive oil and rub all over the cut side of the meat. Season with black pepper. Lay in a shallow dish, cover and leave to marinate in the refrigerator for at least 1 hour, preferably overnight.

The next day, remove from the marinade, reserving the marinade for basting. Barbecue the leg of lamb over medium hot coals for 15–20 minutes, basting, then turn over and cook for a further 20 minutes, basting with a brush of rosemary sprigs from time to time. Alternatively, place the leg of lamb on a foil-lined grill rack and cook under a medium hot grill for 20 minutes, baste then turn over and continue for a further 20 minutes, the meat should be medium.

Once cooked, remove the leg of lamb from the heat, season with salt, then cover loosely with foil and allow to rest for 10 minutes before carving into long thin slices.

There are versions of these all over the region and each one is different. The addition of potato and breadcrumbs are pure Tuscan thrift. Sometimes the meatballs are dipped in flour or even fine polenta before frying.

meatballs with porcini mushrooms and pecorino
polpette toscane

50 g dried porcini mushrooms, soaked in warm water for 30 minutes

300 g minced beef or veal

200 g cooked rice or mashed potato

4 tablespoons freshly grated pecorino cheese

3 tablespoons chopped fresh parsley, plus extra to serve

1 garlic clove, finely chopped

50 g fresh white breadcrumbs

2 tablespoons milk

1 egg, beaten

sea salt and freshly ground black pepper

olive oil, for frying

tomato sauce

2 tablespoons olive oil

1 small onion, finely chopped

two 400 g cans chopped tomatoes, drained

2 tablespoons fresh basil

serves 4

Drain the mushrooms and chop them finely. Put into a bowl with the minced meat, potato, pecorino, parsley and garlic. Mix together well, then soak the breadcrumbs in the milk, squeeze until damp and add the egg. Season with salt and pepper and mix well until it begins to come together. Cover and chill in the refrigerator for 30 minutes.

Meanwhile, to make the tomato sauce, heat the olive oil in a frying pan, add the onion and cook for 5 minutes until softened. Add the tomatoes and basil and simmer for 30 minutes.

Form the chilled meatball mixture into 8 slightly flattened cakes or balls and fry in hot olive oil for about 3 minutes on each side until cooked through and golden brown. Add the tomato sauce and reheat for 5 minutes until boiling. Sprinkle with parsley, then serve immediately.

devilled grilled chicken
pollo alla diavola

Chicken and small gamebirds are very popular cooked this way. They are split open and flattened to cook evenly. Tuscans love to cook *alla brace* – over hot coals in the hearth. To make the charcoal braizier, a wood fire is lit, and when the wood has turned to glowing red ashes, they are spread out in an even layer and left until white on top. A low iron grill on legs is set over the braizier and the spatchcocked birds cooked on top. The smell is wonderful as they sizzle over the coals. The cooked spatchcocked bird is said to resemble the shape of the devil's face, hence the name *alla diavola*. The legs resemble devil's horns, the charring is the colour of the devil and the chilli makes it hotter than hell! The best way to eat these is with your fingers.

1 medium chicken, about 1.5 kg
200 ml olive oil
freshly squeezed juice of 1 lemon
2 garlic cloves, crushed
1 teaspoon hot chilli flakes
sea salt and freshly ground black pepper
lemon wedges, to serve

serves 4

Take the chicken and turn breast side down. You will see the backbone underneath the skin on the base, finishing with the parson's nose! Take a pair of kitchen scissors and cut along one side of the backbone. Cut along the other side and remove the backbone completely. Turn the bird over, breast side uppermost, and open out. Press down hard on the breast bone until you hear a crack and the bird flattens out.

Mix the olive oil with the lemon juice, garlic, chilli flakes and add a good pinch of salt and lots of pepper. Pour this into a shallow dish, add the chicken and turn in the marinade to coat. Cover and leave to marinate in the refrigerator for at least 1 hour, preferably overnight.

Remove the chicken from the refrigerator and marinade and lay it flat on one side of a mesh grill basket. Clamp it shut. Grill or barbecue bone-side first for 20 minutes. Turn over and lower the heat and cook for a further 20–30 minutes until cooked through and blackened, but not burnt. Baste with the marinade from time to time. Serve piping hot with lemon wedges.

A simple way to give ordinary chicken or rabbit all the taste of the wild hills of the interior. The secret is in the reduction of the wine and the long, slow cooking. Farmed rabbits are huge in Italy and come with everything attached, which really adds to the sauce (the heads being quite a delicacy!). Expect this dish to have a rich sauce of tomato, herbs and perhaps mushrooms – all available to the hunter on his trail into the wilds. The sauce is very dark and rich, so serve with plain fare such as polenta or a salad to follow.

1 medium chicken, about 1.5 kg, or 1 large rabbit, head removed and reserved, livers reserved, jointed into 8

4 large garlic cloves, finely chopped

1 tablespoon finely chopped rosemary

1 teaspoon sea salt

1 teaspoon freshly cracked black pepper

25 g dried porcini mushrooms

1 bottle dry red wine

2 sprigs rosemary

3 tablespoons olive oil

2 tablespoons balsamic vinegar

2 tablespoons sun-dried tomato paste or tomato purée

400 g can chopped tomatoes

75 g whole black olives

sea salt and freshly ground black pepper

a little stock or water

chopped fresh parsley, to serve

serves 4

hunter's style rabbit
coniglio alla cacciatora

Wash and dry the chicken or rabbit joints. Mix the garlic, rosemary, and the measured salt and pepper together and rub well into the flesh, especially the cut sides. Cover and allow to marinate for at least 2 hours.

Soak the mushrooms in warm water for at least 20 minutes. Meanwhile pour the wine into a non-corrosive pan, add the rosemary sprigs and boil hard until the wine is reduced by half. Strain and cool.

Heat the oil in a large frying pan and fry the chicken or rabbit (including the heads) until well browned all over, then remove to a casserole. Fry the livers in the frying pan, if using, and add to the chicken or rabbit. Deglaze the pan with the balsamic vinegar, then add the wine, scraping up the sediment. Whisk in the tomato paste, tomatoes and add the mushrooms and their soaking water, season with salt and pepper and bring to the boil. Pour over the chicken or rabbit. Add a little water to bring the liquid up to just cover the joints and add the olives. Bring to the boil then cover and simmer very gently for 45 minutes to 1 hour.

Lift the chicken or rabbit to a warm serving dish. Mash the livers into the sauce and reduce by boiling fast to a syrupy consistency, if necessary. Pour the sauce over the chicken or rabbit and serve sprinkled with parsley.

This is a wonderful way to cook pheasant or guinea fowl when the walnuts are falling off the tree and the grapes are bursting with flavour, also in season are little oranges that are bright green on the outside, but bright orange and sweet on the inside. I've cooked these and eaten them on the terrazzo overlooking the vineyard below. It was early autumn, but it was warm and we could smell the grapes as they were being harvested.

pheasant roasted with vin santo, grapes and walnuts
fagiano al vin santo, uva e noci

6 unwaxed clementines or other small oranges

675 g white or red grapes, plus extra to garnish

20 fresh walnuts in shell, or 125 g walnut halves

30 g dried porcini mushrooms, soaked in warm water for 30 minutes

200 ml Vin Santo

2 young pheasants, plucked, drawn and trussed with giblets*

softened butter, for basting

2 teaspoons balsamic vinegar

sea salt and freshly ground black pepper

pheasant feathers, to decorate, if available

serves 6

Grate the zest from 2 clementines and squeeze the juice from all of them, then place in a bowl, reserving the ungrated squeezed halves. Purée the grapes roughly in a food processor and pour into the clementine juice. Shell the fresh walnuts.

Strain the mushrooms and reserve liquid and finely chop the mushrooms. Pour half the clementine and grape juice into a roasting tin, adding the Vin Santo and any giblets, except the liver. Place the reserved clementine halves inside the pheasant cavities. Spread the pheasants with butter and season with salt and pepper. Place the birds in the roasting tin on one side, legs uppermost. Roast in a preheated oven at 200°C (400°F) Gas 6 for 15 minutes. Turn the birds over on the other side, baste with the pan juices and roast for another 15 minutes. Finally sit the birds upright, baste well and roast for a final 15 minutes or until done. Test by pushing a skewer into the meatiest part of the thigh – the juices should run clear.

Transfer the pheasants to a warmed serving platter and keep warm. Pour the reserved clementine and grape juice into the roasting tin. Stir in the reserved mushroom water, mushrooms and balsamic vinegar. Bring to the boil, scraping up any sediment from the bottom of the roasting pan. Boil for 1–2 minutes, then strain into a saucepan, pressing the juice through the sieve with the back of a wooden spoon. Stir in the walnuts, bring to the boil and reduce the sauce to 450 ml. Taste and season well. The sauce should be slightly syrupy – if not, reduce a little more. Spoon the walnuts around the pheasant and pour the sauce into a warmed sauceboat. Dress the pheasant with grapes and cleaned pheasant feathers, if available. Serve with the sauce.

*Note If your butcher is preparing the birds, ask him to keep the feathers and giblets. Or use chicken or turkey giblets.

prosciutti and cinghiale

There is no avoiding the stern gaze of the bespectacled stuffed boar heads peering down from above the doors of *salumerie* (delicatessens) in Siena. Tuscans love hunting and wild boar (*cinghiale*) is a real favourite. The meat is used in rich stews and pasta sauces and made into all sorts of cured meats, sausages and salamis. It tastes like a gamy version of pork, but the cuts are slightly smaller. Wild boar prosciutto is dark red, salty and drier than *prosciutto crudo*. It tastes particularly good with thick slices of Tuscan bread. The whole leg (ham), including hoof and hair, is cured in salt and masses of black pepper for 4–5 months. Little sausages are made with minced wild boar, pork fat, salt, pepper, garlic and Chianti, aged for a month, then preserved in olive oil.

Once drawn into a *salumeria*, a wonderful adventure in all things piggy awaits. First of all, there is the sweet aroma of salt-cured meats, hams, sausages, salamis and *lardo* (see below). The collective name for these preserved meats is *salumi,* which derives from the Latin word for salted. The name prosciutto derives from the Latin word *perexsuctus*, meaning dry, and in ancient Rome, the shops sold *panis et perna* (bread and prosciutto), the forerunner of porchetta-filled buns in today's markets.

Tuscan ham is known throughout Italy as *prosciutto crudo salato* or *prosciutto saporito*, to distinguish it from *prosciutto di Parma* or *prosciutto dolce*, which is softer and sweeter. It has been awarded a *Denominazione di Origine Protetta (DOP)* (Protected Designation of Origin) to safeguard its unique qualities. Each ham must weigh 11 kilograms and be from a pig that is at least 9 months old. It must be aged for at least one year, usually 14–15 months. The exposed fleshy end at the top of the leg is covered by a thick layer of ground black pepper to preserve it. The dry-cure is flavoured with sea salt, pepper, juniper berries, rosemary and garlic, although individual consortium members may add fennel, wine or vinegar to individualize their ham.

Cutting ham on the bone with a long knife is quite an art. The skin and some fat is trimmed away, then the ham is sliced across the narrow edge of the ham parallel to the bone, keeping the slice as large as possible. Our friend Marcella likes to cut the ham resting in a wooden support with a v-shaped notch to hold the bone in position. She also likes to hold the ham under her arm and carve off slices that way – what a woman!

One of the foundations of a sauce or soup in Tuscan cooking is pancetta, cured belly pork, rather like green or unsmoked streaky bacon. There are many different types, including *pancetta tesa* or *carnesecca*, which looks like a flat slab of bacon; and *arrotolata*, *coppata* and *magretta*, which are rolled pancettas similar to Scottish Ayrshire bacon. There is a smoked version, but it is mainly made in the North. Another Tuscan treasure is a prosciutto made from the *Cinta Senese*, an ancient breed of pig once reared in the Chianti region and enjoying a revival. The pigs are free-range and eat a natural diet, which intensifies the flavour of the meat and fat.

Tuscany produces two distinctive salamis. Intensely flavoured with salt, pepper, garlic and red wine, *salame Toscano* is studded with large pieces of fat and whole peppercorns. *Finocchiona* is made from the fat and lean meat from the pork shoulder and cheek, and is flavoured with fennel seeds, red wine, salt, pepper and herbs. Matured for 6 months, it tends to be larger and more moist, and is cut thickly to prevent it falling apart. Both of these salamis are usually made with three parts lean pork to one of hard pork fat, with salt, pepper and permitted quantities of nitrates to aid preservation and colour. Additional seasonings include garlic, fennel seeds and chilli pepper. Once filled into natural casings, they are hung to dry and age in well-ventilated, dark, cool rooms. The sign of a good-quality salami is a compact filling, where the pockets of fat do not separate from the meat when sliced.

One of the most interesting pork products is *lardo*. This is salt and pepper-cured pork back fat, sold in thick, unctuous white slabs. This was used as cooking fat before our more health-conscious ways with olive oil. It is variously flavoured with rosemary, sage, cloves and cinnamon. It is usually sliced into the thinnest of slivers and laid on hot bruschetta, or simply eaten in paper-thin aromatic slices to melt on the tongue. The king of lardo comes from the village of Colonnata where it is cured for 6 months in special marble basins, giving it a fine flavour and texture.

Soppressata is another delicacy, also known as headcheese or brawn. It is made from cooked chopped pork head meat, tongue and gelatinous skin mixed with salt, pepper, garlic, spices and rosemary. The mix is pressed into a sausage shape, cooled and sliced. No part of the pig remains unused in Tuscan cooking. Even the blood is made into heavily spiced sausages speckled with white fat – *buristo*, *biroldo* and *mallegato* – superior versions of British black pudding. Some localities add raisins and pine nuts.

And last but not least is the fresh pork sausage, part of everyday life. Made from minced shoulder and belly of pork and flavoured with salt, pepper and garlic, it flavours risotto, makes a sauce for pasta and is served with *Fagioli all'Uccelletto* (page 121). Sausages are also grilled as *spiedini* (kebabs) on the embers of a fire. The Tuscans may not be great pig breeders, but they are masters at converting pork into *salumi* that express the very essence of the region and its culture.

Clockwise from top left: leg of Tuscan prosciutto; wild boar head outside a salumeria; salami; selection of cured meats Tuscan pork sausages; slicing the prosciutto; producer's label on the prosciutto.

contorni
vegetable side dishes

market gardens

Tuscany has the luck to be slap bang in the middle of Italy and not only has its own superb produce due to a pretty temperate climate, but also has 'imported' produce from all over Italy and the islands. The climate is so varied from North to South that growing seasons can be 'extended'. Sicily and southern Italy have a hot climate with little or no frost and can supply tomatoes almost year round. Tuscans cook, preserve and bottle according to the seasons. If it is not in season, they don't waste time looking for it. *Contorni* (vegetable accompaniments) are usually simply cooked and served on a separate plate so as not to interfere with the main dish. They are never added to the plate in front of you, but eaten straight from their own plate or dish. They can be served as a separate course in a *frittata*, *tortino* or *sformato*, or simply stuffed. In cooking, their flavours are not disguised, but are enhanced by simple combinations of ingredients – the fewer, the better – often mixing sweet, salt and sour together.

Whether eaten as part of an antipasto; in a soup, main course or salad; or as a dessert, the Tuscan way of preparing fruit or vegetables is always a celebration of the fruit or vegetable itself, bringing out the most in its flavour or texture. You will certainly know when things are in season – take a walk in any daily market or look at changing local menus. The more abundant the produce is, the cheaper it is, and that's when it is bought in bulk, bottled, jammed and preserved for the winter months. This produce is picked at the proper time of year, when perfectly ripe and ready to eat. You cannot escape the year-round *feste* and *sagre* devoted to celebrating each and every edible thing as it comes into peak season – they are great fun, and it is a refreshing sight to see people rejoicing in the bounty of nature.

Orto di Primavera

The *Orto di Primavera* (spring market garden) begins around the end of March and continutes through April and May. Spring brings great excitement in Tuscany – the blossom is on the trees and in the hedgerows, everything is turning luminous green and the earth is warming. The colours in the spring market are white and every shade of green and purple. Easter Saturday is the traditional time to sow vegetables and legumes as the moon is waning *(luna calante)* and horticulture guided by the phases of the moon is a tradition still followed by many.

Asparagus *(asparagi)* in all its guises floods the market stalls – from spindly wild varieties and thin green stems flushed with purple, to every grade of Italy's beloved white asparagus. In April

Clockwise from top left: apple blossom; spinach; Tuscan orchards; hedgerow salad; the market at Montepulciano; broad beans.

and May, the floodgates open to **artichokes** *(carciofi)* of all sizes. Tuscan lore says that the Etruscans cultivated artichokes from the indigenous wild thistle. Part of the artichoke is used as a rennet for making cheese. There are baby artichokes, round Roman ones for stuffing, and elongated ones, still with stalks and leaves on. The best artichokes come from Chiusure, near Siena, where there is an annual festival (page 16) to celebrate them.

Snug in their furry pods, **broad beans** *(buccelli)* are eaten raw at the beginning of the season while they are small and young. They are put into a basket, pods and all, for you to help yourself – the pleasure being both in the podding and eating fresh beans. There are also piles of sweet new **peas** *(piselli)*, again in the pod.

The new **fresh garlic** *(aglio fresco)* is everywhere. Early in the season, before the bulb has developed, you can find thinnings, which are like a cross between a spring onion and a leek and which are delicious chopped up raw in salads or omelettes. Later on, there are big fat heads of tender young cloves with a mild creamy texture. There are bunches of fat **spring onions** *(cipolline)* and, if you are lucky, **wild salad leaves** *(insalata di campo)*, tender cultivated salad leaves and wild hop shoots, cooked and eaten like young asparagus. Springy young **spinach** *(spinaci)* seems to burst out of wooden crates, begging to be cleaned and cooked.

Wild fennel *(finocchio selvatico)* starts to grow by the roadside, where it will flower then turn to seed. The flower-heads are gathered when in full blossom, then quickly dried and ground into a fantastic greenish-yellow pungent anise-flavoured powder to perfume chicken, fish, rabbit, pork and ham dishes. Fennel seeds are used too, but the flavour is not as special. **Rosemary** *(rosmarino)* is covered with fluffy intense blue flowers and **sage** *(salvia)* is beginning to regrow.

Orto d'Estate

In the *Orto d'Estate* (summer market garden), which lasts from the end of May to August, the market changes colour to all shades of reds, darker greens and golds. *Pinzimonio*, an olive oil dip seasoned with salt and pepper, is served with fresh raw seasonal vegetables for dipping and makes a great summer starter or appetizer to have with drinks.

Tomatoes *(pomodori)* were almost unknown in Tuscany until Garibaldi brought them back from Sicily during the Unification of Italy in the mid-19th century. They have now become ubiquitous and are in abundance at this time of year. There are huge, knobbly ones, in hues of green and red for salads, and long, firm ones for conserving and bottling whole *(pomodori pelati)*. Soft, ripe red ones are used to make *sugo* (sauce), while others are perfect for making *Pappa al Pomodoro* (page 36) and *Panzanella* (page 23). When at

their peak, tomatoes are bought to make a puréed tomato sauce for winter, known as *passata* or *conserva di pomodoro*, or to make *concentrato di pomodoro* (concentrated tomato paste).

Also in the markets, you will find tortured red and yellow **peppers** *(peperoni)*, round and long **aubergines** *(melanzane)*, **courgettes** *(zucchini)* and bunches of fresh **red chillies** *(peperoncini)* pleading to be taken home. Coquettish bunches of golden courgette flowers, picked early in the morning, preen themselves amongst a sea of mysterious salad greens and shy purply red radicchio. Waxy **new potatoes** *(patate novelle)* lie side by side with green-shrouded **sweetcorn** *(granturco dolce)*. Follow your nose to find **basil** *(basilico)* for planting into pots to bask in the summer sunshine and perfume a balcony and perky bouquets of aromatic continental **parsley** *(prezzemolo)*.

The 'holy' trinity of crunchy orange **carrots** *(carote)*, firm, juicy **onions** *(cipolle)* and serenely blowsy **celery** *(sedano)* are just asking to be chopped up and gently fried in fragrant olive oil as a *soffritto*. There are fine **green beans** *(fagiolini verdi)* and, later on, fresh **cannellini beans** followed by fuschia and ivory splashed pods of **borlotti beans**.

Jewel-like **cherries** *(ciliege)* tumble temptingly beside the summer-long advance of **strawberries** *(fragole)*, which are often served sliced into red wine, and in June tiny fragrant wild strawberries appear. Neat rows of perfectly ripe **apricots** *(albicocche)*, **peaches** *(pesci)* and **nectarines** *(peschenoce)* sit beside **cantaloupe melons** *(meloni cantalupi)* ready for eating with prosciutto, and red and green **watermelons** *(angurie)* are stacked in fragrant mountains.

If all this is not enough, dessert **grapes** *(uva fragola)*, tasting of strawberries start to appear in late summer with exotic muscat grapes and **figs** *(fichi)* from palest almond green to violet black. Towards the end of the season, there may be a few fresh milky **almonds** *(mandorle)* and **green olives** *(olive verdi)* for brining.

Orto d'Autunno

The *Orto d'Autunno* (autumn market garden) in September and October marks the beginning of the wild mushroom *(funghi)* season, which lasts until the first frosts. Tuscans are mad for them and will scavenge the bosky countryside at any opportunity. You can only pick up to 2 kilograms per day by law, however, and there are strict gudelines to prevent the smallest being taken. The most coveted is the *porcino* or French cep (bot. *Boletus edulis*). The best fresh porcini are thinly sliced and eaten raw in a salad, but my favourite way with a large meaty mushroom is to brush the cap with good-quality olive oil and grill it over a wood fire like a steak. Porcini mushrooms are also sliced and dried for use during the winter months.

There are numerous other mushrooms which can be found in local markets and surrounding areas at this time of year, such as **field mushrooms** *(pratolini)*, pretty yellow and orange **chanterelles** *(gallinaci)* and **hedgehog mushrooms** *(steccherini* or *dentini d'orati)*, pale, suede-like mushrooms with downy spines on the underside. If you are lucky, you may come across the coveted, egg-like **Caesar's mushroom** *(ovole)*, a delicacy prized since Roman times which only grows in open deciduous woodland. **Puffballs** *(puzzarelle)*, including giant ones, can be found along with **parasol mushrooms** *(caroce)* and **wood blewits** *(ordinale viola* or *agarico violetto)*. There is also a type of **russula** *(rossola)* called *biete* and the small, delicately bundled **honey fungus** *(chiodini)*, known as 'little nails'.

It is always advisable to have your mushrooms checked by a local expert as some can be poisonous or even deadly. The local chemist may be able to check them or will be able to direct you to someone who can. If in any doubt at all, do not eat them. The wild herb locally known as *mentuccia* or *nepitella* is often put into the bag when you buy mushrooms. It grows all over the place and is a sort of wild catmint, resembling a cross between mint and oregano.

During autumn, **maize** *(mais* or *granturco)* is harvested for animal feed and dried and ground for polenta. There are also majestic, sculptural, brown **pumpkins** *(zucca)* with intense orange flesh to fill ravioli and roast in the oven, that can be stored throughout the winter, as well as all sorts of squash.

There are **apples** *(mele)* galore to make *Torta di Mele* and **pears** *(pere)* of all shapes – long and thin, short and fat – encased in burnished gold and blushing to be partnered by an aged pecorino. **Walnuts** *(noci)* are dropping off the trees, and there are

plums (*susine*), **loquats** (*nespole*) and **persimmons** (*kaki*). Finally, October sees the start of the *vendemmia* (grape harvest) for making wine and grappa.

Orto d'Inverno

During the *Orto d'Inverno* (winter market garden), which lasts from November to February, **pomegranates** (*melograni*) start to burst open to reveal their ruby treasure and **olives** (*olive*) begin to be harvested to make oil. The market overflows with **Swiss chard** (*bietole*), **spinach** (*spinaci*), **escarole** (*cicoria*), **chicory** (*endivia*), **radicchio** (*radicchio*), long dark green plumes of Tuscan **winter cabbage** (*cavolo nero*), **cauliflowers** (*cavolfiori*) of all colours, **purple sprouting broccoli** (*broccoletti di rape*) and many other unfamiliar brassicas. Piles of silvery grey **cardoons** (*cardi* or *gobbi*), tenderized by the first frosts, and looking like ancient unshaven celery, lie waiting to reveal their artichoke-tasting stems after long and careful preparation.

Chestnuts (*castagne*) are gathered and grilled on the fire in a *briscia* – a sort of frying pan punctured with holes – and there are special evenings and *sagras* in local bars celebrating roasted chestnuts and the rough new wine. Chestnuts are also dried and ground into wonderfully delicious and fine *farina di castagne*, once the 'polenta' of the Tuscan peasant farmer.

In November, there are two **truffle** fairs (*fiere del tartufo*) in Tuscany – one at San Miniato, Pisa, and one at San Giovanni d'Asso, Siena. Truffles, truffle dogs, truffle menus, truffle products, truffle-seeking contests and more truffles! Truffles are usually shaved thinly on a special mini mandoline. They are shaved directly onto a warm or hot dish so that the heady flavour and aroma is released. White truffles are shaved over risotto, delicate pasta dishes, or cheese dishes. Black truffles are delicious with eggs, polenta and in stronger sauces.

I have been lucky enough to be in Tuscany many times in late autumn when the Supreme Emperors of Funghi – black and white truffles – are around. But visiting San Giovanni d'Asso for the first time in April, I was amazed to discover that there was still a delicious fresh truffle being served in many local restaurants. With a little further research, I have collated the following table – it seems there are truffles of varying colours and pungency from June, through summer, autumn and winter all the way through to April. The dates given below are approximate as seasons vary depending on the weather.

10 September to 31 December

    White truffle (*tartufo bianco*); bot. *Tuber magnatum pico*. This is the most highly prized truffle in Italy and is consequently very expensive. The delicious, but volatile, taste and smell of white truffles are like decayed compost: earthy, sweetly nutty and pungent. You either love them or hate them!

15 November to 15 March

    Black or **Périgord truffle** (*tartufo di Norcia* or *tartufo di Spoleto* or *tartufo di pregiato*); bot. *Tuber melanosporum vitt*. This is another favourite, but more robust than the delicate white truffle.

15 November to 30 April

    Black winter or muscat truffle (*tartufo nero d'inverno, trifola nera* or *tartufo nero moscato*); bot. *Tuber brumale var. moscatum* or *Tuber brumale vitt*.

1 October to 31 December

    Burgundy or grey truffle (*scorzone* or *tartufo di Fragno*); bot. *Tuber uncinatum chatin*.

10 January to 30 April

    Whitish truffle (*tartufo bianchetto marzuolo*); bot. *Tuber tobinum pico*.

1 June to 30 November

    Summer truffle (*tartufo scorzone*); bot. *Tuber aestivum vitt*.

1 September to 31 December

    Smooth black truffle (*tartufo nero liscio*); bot. *Tuber macrosporum vitt*.

1 September to 31 January

    Bagnoli truffle (*tartufo nero ordinario*); bot. *Tuber mesentericum vitt*.

Left to right: the market at Montepulciano; bunches of basil; sage plants; broad beans; artichokes; aubergines; a tomato stall; fresh and dried porcini mushrooms; truffles.

The Tuscans consider themselves the greatest hunters in Italy. In the past, when they used to cook *uccelletti* (little gamebirds), they would generally season them with salt, pepper and sage. Although this dish contains no *uccelletti*, it still reminds us of this tradition because it has sage in it. This is the most famous of the hundreds of ways to cook beans in the region. Taste your sage before using as garden-grown can be quite strong and overpowering as opposed to hothouse sage.

beans cooked with tomato, garlic and sage
fagioli all'uccelletto

1 kg fresh toscanelli, cannellini or borlotti beans, or 450 g dried beans

350 g fresh ripe tomatoes, peeled and deseeded or 350 ml Italian sieved tomatoes *(passata)*

90 ml extra virgin olive oil

3 garlic cloves, crushed

about 12 fresh sage leaves

sea salt and freshly ground black pepper

serves 6

If using dried beans, soak them in water for 6–7 hours or overnight. Then drain and rinse them and cook them in plenty of simmering water until soft, about 1–1½ hours, then drain. If using fresh beans, shell and boil them in slightly salted water until ready, 25–30 minutes, then drain.

If using fresh tomatoes, blend to a purée in a food processor and put to one side. Heat the oil in a pan and add the garlic, 4–6 sage leaves and a sprinkling of pepper. Fry until the garlic is golden, then add the cooked beans, the puréed tomatoes or *passata* and the remaining sage leaves. Simmer for 10 minutes or until the beans are just starting to crumble and the mixture slightly thickened. Check that the beans are well enough seasoned with salt and pepper before serving. These are great with really meaty sausages.

Beans were traditionally cooked this way, in a Chianti flask *(fiasco spagliato)* blown from one piece of glass. The flask was embedded in the dying embers of the hearth to cook for as long as possible. Moulded flasks with a join will not work for this dish as they can crack in the heat. You can use a casserole in the oven, however, even if it is not as romantic! The beans emerge deliciously creamy and are best served hot with Italian sausages, roast pork or as a simple first course with bread and a few anchovies. Toscanelli beans are traditional for this dish as they are small and won't stick in the neck of the flask, but they are hard to find. Tuscans say that when cooked, the beans have a particular perfume.

beans simmered in a chianti flask
fagioli nel fiasco

400 g small dried cannellini or navy beans (very small white beans)

2 garlic cloves

6–8 sage leaves

10 tablespoons extra virgin olive oil, plus extra to serve

sea salt and freshly ground black pepper

a hand-blown Chianti flask (optional)

serves 4

Put the dry beans into the Chianti flask or an earthenware casserole or bean pot. Add the garlic, sage leaves, olive oil, and a little salt and pepper. Pour in enough warm water to fill the flask three-quarters full – or three times the volume of the beans of water, if using a casserole. Plug the neck of the flask with scrunched up greaseproof paper or a stopper of rolled and folded muslin – this allows the contents to 'breathe' and stops the flask exploding! Wrap the flask in a clean tea towel. If using a casserole or bean pot, make sure it has a tight-fitting lid.

Put the flask in a bain-marie and cook in the oven for 3 hours, turning every now and then to distribute the beans, water and heat. Put the covered casserole in the oven and check after 2 hours, then put a circle of greaseproof paper directly on top of the beans inside the casserole to keep in the moisture, then cover and return to the oven for another hour. The beans must be very tender and should absorb most of the water and oil.

When they are cooked, pour the beans into a heated serving dish and dress liberally with olive oil, then season to taste with salt and pepper. Serve hot.

Did you know that the flowers we often see with a small courgette attached are the female flowers, and the ones that are really for stuffing are the male flowers? They are sold in sunny yellow bunches in early summer in most Italian markets and are very fragile and must be cooked straight away. They needn't be stuffed, of course, but they make a gorgeous appetizer.

stuffed courgette flowers with ricotta and mint
fiori di zucchini ripieni

12 courgette flowers

filling
250 g fresh ricotta
finely grated zest of ½ unwaxed lemon
1 tablespoon chopped fresh mint

batter
250 g plain flour
100 ml extra virgin olive oil
350 ml warm water
2 egg whites
sea salt and freshly ground black pepper
vegetable oil, for deep-frying

a deep-fryer

makes 12

To make the batter, put the flour and 1 teaspoon salt into a bowl and make a well in the centre. Mix the olive oil with the warm water and pour into the well. Mix the batter until smooth, then leave it to rest for at least 1 hour.

Meanwhile to make the filling, mix the ricotta with the lemon zest, mint, salt and pepper.

Beat the egg whites until stiff and fold into the rested batter. Heat the oil in a deep-fryer or wok to 190°C (375°F) – a piece of stale bread dropped in should turn golden in a few seconds. Remove any small pistils from inside the flowers, the stalks and any leaves on the outside. Place a small teaspoonful of stuffing in each flower and gently fold or twist the petals around it. Drop 4 stuffed flowers at a time into the batter, gently shake off the excess, then fry until golden brown. Drain thoroughly on crumpled kitchen paper and serve immediately sprinkled with salt. Repeat with the remaining flowers. These stuffed courgette flowers don't like to hang around for long – not that they will!

spinach with eggs and cream
spinaci con uove

This is my version of a famous Florentine dish of spinach and béchamel sauce baked with eggs. Although delicious, I think you can taste the spinach and fresh farm eggs much better when cooked with cream instead of the sauce. A good grating of nutmeg is essential here, and plenty of salt and pepper.

1 kg fresh spinach
50 g butter
250 ml cream
4 eggs
freshly grated nutmeg
3 tablespoons freshly grated Parmesan cheese
sea salt and freshly ground black pepper

serves 4

Pull the stalks off the spinach leaves then wash very well in plenty of cold water, then chop roughly. Melt the butter in a large pan, add the spinach and cook until wilted. Lift out the spinach and drain through a colander, catching any juices than run out.

Arrange the spinach in a buttered baking dish. Carefully pour over the cream, then make 4 indentations in the spinach and crack an egg in each one. Pour the collected spinach juices back into the pan and boil to reduce. Season with salt, pepper and nutmeg and pour over the cream and spinach. Finally, sprinkle with Parmesan and bake in a preheated oven at 200°C (400°F) Gas 6 for 15–20 minutes or until the eggs have set and the whole dish is bubbling.

peas with prosciutto
piselli al prosciutto

Fresh peas almost need no cooking at all, and this dish makes the most of their freshness. If I have time, I like to make use of the pea pods which are bursting with flavour, so I make a quick pea stock to give the dish extra flavour. Add more stock if the dish looks dry – there should be plenty of sweet, buttery juices. This is also a good way with frozen peas, which are after all peas picked in their prime and fast frozen.

1 kg fresh peas in their pods (to give about 500 g podded weight)
150 g thickly sliced Italian ham, such as Parma ham, Serrano ham or pancetta
50 g butter
1 small onion, finely chopped
sea salt and freshly ground black pepper

serves 4

Pod the peas, reserving the pods and peas separately. Roughly chop the pods, put them into a saucepan, barely cover with water and bring to the boil. Simmer for 10 minutes, strain and set aside.

Slice the prosciutto into thin strips. Melt the butter in a medium saucepan, add the onion and cook gently for 5 minutes until softening but not colouring. Add the fresh peas and 100 ml pea stock, and salt and pepper to taste. Stir well, then cover and simmer for 5 minutes. Uncover and stir in the prosciutto. Cook over a moderate heat for a couple of minutes then serve immediately.

pumpkin roasted with sage and onion
zucca arrostita con cipolle e salvia

750 g fresh butternut squash pumpkin

6 tablespoons extra virgin olive oil

2 large onions, sliced

12 fresh sage leaves

a pinch of chilli flakes

1 tablespoon red wine vinegar or balsamic vinegar

sea salt and freshly ground black pepper

serves 4

Pumpkin is a favourite vegetable throughout Italy, and is generally made into soup or ravioli filling. However, if the flesh is not too watery, it is delicious roasted in olive oil on a bed of sage and sliced onions.

Scoop the seeds out of the squash and cut away the skin. Cut into long slices or chunks. Pour 4 tablespoons olive oil into a metal or enamel roasting tin and add the onion. Season with salt and pepper and toss well to coat. Scatter the pumpkin over the onion and the sage leaves over the pumpkin. Drizzle with the remaining olive oil and season with chilli flakes, salt and pepper. Roast in a preheated oven at 220°C (425°F) Gas 7 for 25–30 minutes until tender and beginning to brown. Remove from the oven, sprinkle with the vinegar while it is still hot, then serve.

potatoes baked with wine and mushrooms
patate e funghi al forno

Baking sliced potatoes with mushrooms in layers allows the potatoes to absorb the juices and earthy flavour of the funghi. Try to use the darkest mushrooms you can for this as they will have the best taste – Tuscans would use wild porcini in season. You can always mix fresh with reconstituted dried mushrooms for a more intense flavour.

Peel the potatoes and slice thickly. Add to a bowl of cold water as you go. Trim and slice the mushrooms thickly. Heat the olive oil in a large frying pan and add the mushrooms and garlic. Fry for abut 5 minutes until beginning to brown. Stir in the parsley. Put a layer of half the potatoes in the bottom of a deep gratin dish, drizzle with olive oil, and cover this with a layer of half the mushrooms, seasoning as you go. Cover with a layer of the remaining potatoes, drizzle with olive oil, then add a layer of the remaining mushrooms and drizzle with oil. Pour in the wine, cover with foil and bake in a preheated oven at 180°C (350°F) Gas 4 for 30 minutes. Uncover and cook for a further 30 minutes or until the potatoes are completely tender.

Note To cut the cooking time in two, blanche the sliced potatoes in boiling salted water for 5 minutes before layering up.

900 g medium–sized potatoes

700 g flavoursome mushrooms such as dark flat cap, chestnut or portobello field mushrooms (or fresh wild mushrooms if you can find them)

200 ml extra virgin olive oil, plus extra for drizzling

2 garlic cloves, finely chopped

4 tablespoons chopped fresh parsley

100 ml dry white wine or vermouth

sea salt and freshly ground black pepper

a deep gratin dish

serves 4

braised whole globe artichokes
carciofi ritti di Marcella

Ritti literally means upright or standing to attention, and this is the best way to prepare them when you've got all that Tuscan olive oil to use up. This is a much better alternative to the usual boiled artichokes, as the bases gently fry in the fragrant oil whilst the leaves steam in the vapour. Florentines use a variety of artichoke known as *mamme* – they are large and sometimes have a baby artichoke attached to the same stalk. Sometimes pancetta and parsley are added to the oil, but I prefer them as nature intended, so that the full flavour of artichoke and oil can be appreciated.

2 lemons, sliced
6 globe artichokes, with stems if possible
100 ml extra virgin olive oil, plus extra to serve
sea salt and freshly ground black pepper

serves 6

First prepare the artichokes. Fill a big bowl with water, and add the lemon slices to acidulate it. To prepare the artichokes, starting at the base, snap off all the really tough outer leaves, then snip off the tough tips of the remaining leaves. Slice off the stalks close to the base and put each artichoke in the lemony water until needed to stop them discolouring. Using a potato peeler, peel the stems, dropping them into the water as you go – the stems are just as delicious as the base of the artichokes. Drain the artichokes thoroughly, then turn them upside-down and smack each one lightly with the flat of your hand to slightly separate the leaves. Stand them upright in a large deep saucepan that they will fit snugly in.

Pour the olive oil into the saucepan and set over a medium heat. Season them with salt and pepper and cover the pan. Let them cook for about 15 minutes until the bottoms are nicely browned. Pour in about 150 ml water, bring to the boil, re-cover and simmer very gently for another 20–25 minutes until really tender – a leaf should pull away with little or no resistance. Serve with the pan juices and extra olive oil, salt and pepper.

artichoke and pecorino omelette
frittata ai carciofi

In spring, when artichokes are literally rolling off the market stalls in Tuscany, the new young pecorino cheese appears with the first of the spring pasture milk. The combination of sharp, yet creamy, sheep's cheese and the fresh, almost musky flavour of artichoke hearts is sublime. All this coupled with an omelette made with the most yellow hen's eggs you ever saw makes a perfect lunch. I often double the amount of cheese as I love it so much!

3 large ripe lemons
12 medium purply-green artichokes with stems, heads about 10 cm long
4 tablespoons extra virgin olive oil
6 large eggs
4 tablespoons chopped fresh parsley
4 tablespoons freshly grated pecorino
sea salt and freshly ground black pepper

serves 4

First prepare the artichokes. Fill a big bowl with water, halve the lemons and squeeze in the juice of 4 halves to acidulate it. Use the remaining lemon halves to rub the cut portions of each artichoke as you work. Trim the artichokes by snapping off the dark green and purple outer leaves, starting at the base, and leaving only the pale interior leaves. Trim the stalk down to about 5 cm in length. Trim away the dark green outer layer at the base and peel the fibrous outside of the stalk. Cut about 1 cm off the tip of each artichoke. Put each artichoke in the lemony water until needed to stop them discolouring.

Drain the artichokes, halve them and pat dry. Heat the oil in a large frying pan and sauté the artichokes for 5–10 minutes until tender and golden. Remove from the heat.

Beat the eggs in a bowl, add the parsley and season with salt and pepper. Put the pan back on the heat and pour the eggs around the artichokes. Cook over a gentle heat until almost set. Scatter the pecorino on top and finish off under the grill. Serve warm or at room temperature.

sweet and sour cabbage
verza all'aceto

There are other cabbages apart from *cavolo nero* in this region and all recipes are very simple. One of my favourites is a cabbage called *cavolo verzo*, the nearest equivalent being savoy cabbage or even spring greens. The secret with cabbage is not to cook it for too long.

1 medium savoy cabbage
3 tablespoons olive oil
½ onion, finely chopped
2 tablespoons white wine vinegar
sea salt and freshly ground black pepper

serves 6

Pull off the outside leaves from the cabbage and wash them thoroughly. Halve the cabbage and cut out the core. Shred the cabbage finely. Heat the oil in a large sauté pan and add the onion, cooking for 5 minutes until golden. Add the cabbage and stir to coat with the oil, season with salt and pepper then cover and cook over a gentle heat for 10 minutes. To finish, remove the lid, add the vinegar and raise the heat until it evaporates. Serve immediately.

dolci e postpasti
sweet things

soft almond biscuits from siena
ricciarelli

These delicate biscuits, with their soft almond centres, are said to resemble the almond-shaped eyes of the Madonna in Renaissance paintings. They are associated with the Feast of the Annunciation (March 25th) and, consequently, with fertility. They are also sometimes known as 'nun's thighs'! Use whole blanched almonds, if you can, as they are fresher this way.

175 g whole blanched almonds, ground, or 175 g ground almonds
200 g caster sugar, plus extra for rolling
½ teaspoon baking powder
1 tablespoon plain flour
2 large egg whites
3 drops almond essence
icing sugar, to serve

makes about 16

Put the almonds in a bowl with the sugar. Sift the baking powder with the flour into the almonds and sugar. Whisk the egg whites until stiff but not dry, then stir into the almond mixture. Add the almond essence and blend until you have a soft malleable paste.

Pour some caster sugar onto a plate. Roll heaped tablespoons of the mixture into small balls, roll in the sugar, and then press into the traditional oval or diamond shape by rolling into a fat sausage, tapering the ends, then flattening slightly with the palm of your hand. Put the ricciarelli on a baking sheet lined with baking parchment. Bake in a preheated oven at 200°C (400°F) Gas 6 for 10–12 minutes until lightly golden. Do not overbake or they will be too hard. Remove to a wire rack to cool. Press the tops into icing sugar or simply roll in icing sugar and serve piled high on a plate.

spiced biscuits with candied orange and walnuts
cavallucci

These spicy, crunchy biscuits are a speciality from Siena and at one time were thought to have the image of a horse stamped on the surface, in the tradition of the *Palio* (Siena horse race). They keep well in an airtight container.

200 g caster sugar
100 ml clear honey, such as chestnut honey
200 g walnut pieces, chopped
85 g candied orange peel, finely diced
½ teaspoon powdered aniseed
½ teaspoon cinnamon
¼ teaspoon powdered cloves
500 g plain white flour
1 sachet baking powder
icing sugar, to dust

makes 16

Put the sugar and honey in a saucepan with 200 ml water. Stir and heat gently until dissolved, then boil to the 'thread' stage. Remove from the heat and stir in the walnuts, orange peel and spices.

Sift the flour with the baking powder and spices in a bowl, then pour in the walnut and orange peel mixture and fold into the flour. Tip out and knead the dough – it should be quite firm. Divide into 16 pieces and roll into rough balls, whilst still warm. Put on a floured baking sheet and bake in a preheated oven at 180°C (350°F) Gas 4 for 20–25 minutes until puffed and set but not browned. Dust with icing sugar before serving.

300 g Italian chestnut flour

2 tablespoons pine nuts

50 g walnuts, chopped

150 g raisins, soaked overnight in warm Vin Santo, if liked

a pinch of sea salt

150 ml extra virgin olive oil

150 ml Vin Santo

a few fresh rosemary leaves

Gorgonzola cheese, to serve

a 25 cm shallow ovenproof dish or cake tin

serves 10

This is a very well-known cake in Tuscany, especially in the Lucca region. There are several variations – you can add walnuts or orange peel or more or less olive oil. Some people prefer the castagnaccio very shallow and crunchy; others prefer it thicker, about 2 cm deep. Alternatively, you can mix the flour only with water and sprinkle the rosemary, raisins, pine nuts and walnuts over the batter in the baking dish.

chestnut cake with rosemary, pine nuts and raisins
castagnaccio

Mix the chestnut flour, pine nuts, walnuts and raisins (drained, if soaked in Vin Santo) and a pinch of salt together in a bowl. Stir in 100 ml olive oil, the Vin Santo and enough water – about 200 ml – to make a rather liquid batter, like double cream, and stir well with a whisk, to eliminate any lumps.

Oil a 25 cm shallow ovenproof dish or cake tin. Pour in the mixture to a depth of about 1 cm. Sprinkle the top with rosemary leaves and with a little olive oil. Bake in a preheated oven at 180°C (350°F) Gas 4 for about 30 minutes or until the top layer has become crisp and cracked like a dried riverbed. Serve warm or cold with Gorgonzola.

ricotta and acacia blossom honey ice cream
gelato di ricotta e miele d'acacia

This is a very delicate ice cream with a slight granular texture of ricotta. Chestnut honey has quite a powerful flavour, so I temper it with a hint of vanilla. Chestnuts are a great favourite in this area, and it's not only the French who make *marrons glacés*.

450 g fresh ricotta
100 g acacia honey
600 ml semi-skimmed milk
1 vanilla pod, split
candied chestnuts, to serve

an ice cream maker

makes about 1.5 litres

Put the ricotta and honey in a food processor and blend until smooth. Scrape out into a medium saucepan and whisk in the milk and the split vanilla pod. Bring slowly up to the boil, stirring occasionally, remove from heat and let it infuse for l0 minutes. Shake the vanilla pod around in the liquid to flush out the seeds! Remove the vanilla pod and pour the ricotta mixture through a fine sieve or strainer into a bowl, cool and refrigerate for at least 1 hour or overnight.

When thoroughly chilled, transfer to an ice cream maker and freeze according to the manufacturer's instructions. If necessary, do this in 2 batches, keeping one batch refrigerated while freezing the other batch. Spoon into a chilled container. Cover and freeze for at least 4 hours until firm. Remove to the refrigerator for 30 minutes before serving to soften. Serve in scoops or freeze in individual moulds with the candied chestnuts.

chocolate sorbet
sorbetto al cioccolato

A beautifully smooth, very dark and rich chocolate sorbet which is exquisite eaten with amarena cherries and a blob of whipped cream. As this is a very soft sorbet, make it well in advance and allow it to firm up in the freezer, overnight if possible, before serving.

150 g packed soft dark brown sugar
200 g caster sugar
65 g unsweetened cocoa powder, sifted
50 g dark chocolate (70% cocoa solids), finely chopped or grated
2½ teaspoons vanilla essence
1 teaspoon instant espresso coffee powder

to serve
amarena cherries in syrup
whipped cream
amaretti biscuits

an ice cream maker

makes about 900 ml

Mix 500 ml water, both the sugars and cocoa in a saucepan. Bring slowly to the boil, and cook for 4–5 minutes, whisking until the sugar dissolves. Reduce the heat and simmer for 3 minutes. Remove from the heat and stir in the chocolate, vanilla and espresso powder until melted and dissolved. Cool and chill in the refrigerator.

When thoroughly chilled, transfer to an ice cream maker and freeze according to the manufacturer's instructions. If necessary, do this in 2 batches, keeping one batch refrigerated while freezing the other batch. Spoon into a chilled container. Cover and freeze for at least 4 hours until firm. Remove to the refrigerator for 30 minutes before serving to soften. Serve in scoops with a spoonful of amarena cherries, a blob of whipped cream, and some amaretti biscuits.

A traditional Christmas treat from Siena, panpepato's origins are deeply rooted in the Renaissance spice trade. This dark version of the more familiar *Panforte*, is packed with honey and spices, candied fruits and nuts, and chocolatey cocoa. Perfect to serve after dinner in thin wedges with *'un buon caffè'*. I like to make smaller versions and wrap them in waxed paper tied with rough string and sealing wax as presents. Buy candied fruits in large pieces and chop them up for this – the ready-chopped peel we use for Christmas cakes just won't do, this is a luxury cake!

honey and spice cake
panpepato

100 g walnut halves

100 g whole skinned hazelnuts

100 g blanched almonds

100 g candied orange peel

100 g candied citron peel

50 g plain white flour

4 tablespoons cocoa powder

½ teaspoon ground coriander or whole fennel seeds

1 teaspoon freshly ground black pepper

½ teaspoon ground nutmeg

¼ teaspoon ground cloves

1 teaspoon ground cinnamon

100 g caster sugar

225 g clear honey

25 g unsalted butter

3 tablespoons icing sugar, sifted with ¼ teaspoon each ground nutmeg, cinnamon, black pepper and cloves, for dusting

rice paper

vegetable oil, for oiling

a 20 cm springform cake tin, lightly buttered

makes one 20 cm cake

Line the base and sides of the springform tin with rice paper.

Spread the nuts on a baking tray and bake in a preheated oven at 180°C (350°F) Gas 4 for 10–15 minutes until golden brown. Cool slightly then roughly chop and transfer into a medium bowl. Turn the oven down to 150°C (300°F) Gas 2.

Finely chop the orange and citron peel and stir into the nuts. Sift in the flour, cocoa and spices.

Put the sugar, honey and butter in a saucepan and heat gently, stirring occasionally until dissolved. Boil until the syrup reaches the 'soft ball' stage 117°C–120°C (242°F–248°F) on a sugar thermometer. Quickly stir in the nut mixture and pour into the prepared tin. Smooth the surface with an oiled potato masher. Work quickly before the mixture sets. Bake in the oven for 35 minutes. The cake will not brown or set at this stage. Remove from the oven and set the tin on a cooling rack to cool until firm. The cake will harden as it cools. When cold, remove the tin and trim the rice paper. Dust with the spiced icing sugar. Serve in thin slices.

Note This will keep for 1 month in an airtight tin.

The word *schiacciata* literally means 'flattened'. *Schiacciata con l'uva* is a flatbread baked with the Chianti grape (Sangiovese) and sugar, and is only seen in bakers' shops at grape harvest time. My sweeter, richer version involves black table grapes, walnuts, butter and brown sugar. You could use cherries and pine nuts or even blueberries. Failing all this, soak raisins in Vin Santo or sherry instead of grapes.

sticky grape and walnut focaccia
schiacciata con l'uva

yeast dough

25 g fresh yeast, 1 tablespoon dried active yeast or 1 sachet fast-action dried yeast

a pinch of sugar

500 g plain white flour, plus extra for dusting

2 egg yolks

2 tablespoons olive oil

½ teaspoon sea salt

walnut butter

175 g butter, softened

125 g demerara sugar, plus extra for dusting

finely grated zest of 1 unwaxed lemon

100 g walnuts, chopped

250 g black grapes, deseeded (Sangiovese wine grapes, if possible)

Vin Santo cream

450 ml double cream or mascarpone

3 tablespoons icing sugar

100 ml Vin Santo

a buttered Swiss roll tin

serves 6

If using fresh yeast, mix with the sugar in a medium bowl, then whisk in 250 ml warm water. Leave for 10 minutes until frothy. For dried yeasts, use according to the manufacturer's instructions.

To make the yeast dough, sift the flour into a large bowl and make a well in the centre. Pour in the yeast mixture, egg yolks, olive oil and salt. Mix together until the dough comes together. Tip out onto a lightly floured work surface. Wash and dry your hands and knead for 10 minutes until smooth and elastic. The dough should be quite soft, but if too soft to handle, add more flour. Place in a clean oiled bowl, cover with a damp tea towel and leave to rise until doubled – about 1 hour.

Meanwhile, to make the walnut butter, cream the butter and sugar together with the lemon zest, then stir in the walnuts. Keep at room temperature. When risen, knock the dough back. Shape into a ball, flatten and roll out into a rectangle to line the prepared swiss roll tin. Spread with the walnut butter and grapes and dust with sugar. Cover with a damp cloth and leave to rise for another hour or until puffy and doubled in size. Uncover and bake in the oven at 200°C (400°F) Gas 6 for 15 minutes then turn the oven down to 180°C (350°F) Gas 4 for another 20 minutes or until well risen and golden brown. Allow to cool slightly before turning out. Meanwhile, to make the Vin Santo cream, whisk the cream, icing sugar and Vin Santo together in a bowl until the mixture forms soft peaks. Serve the focaccia cut into wedges with the Vin Santo cream.

In past times, buccellato was made for every christening, now it is always available in the better *pasticcerie* in and around Lucca. It is sometimes served as a dessert – slices are soaked in Vin Santo and covered with strawberries. I think it is delcious toasted for breakfast.

raisin and aniseed cake
buccellato

20 g fresh yeast
150 ml milk, warmed
400 g plain white flour, plus extra for dusting
115 g caster sugar
2 eggs, beaten
50 ml Vin Santo or Marsala
50 g butter, melted
finely grated zest of 1 unwaxed lemon
1 teaspoon aniseed
50 g raisins
sea salt
extra egg white, to glaze

a 20.5 cm ring mould

makes one 20.5 cm cake

Mix the yeast with the warm milk until dissolved then allow to stand. Sift the flour into a bowl and mix with the sugar and a pinch of salt. Make a well in the centre and add the yeast mixture, eggs, Vin Santo, melted butter, lemon zest and aniseed. Mix together with a round-bladed knife until the dough begins to come together. The dough should be very soft. Turn out onto a floured surface and knead for 10 minutes until smooth and elastic. Knead in the raisins. Roll into a long sausage and place in the base of a 20.5 cm ring mould pushing the ends together. Cover with a damp tea towel and leave to rise in a warm place for 1½ hours until doubles in size.

Beat the egg white with a little salt until loose. Uncover the cake and brush the top with the glaze. Bake in a preheated oven at 180ºC (350ºC) Gas 4 for 45 minutes or until risen and deep golden brown. Leave to cool in the tin and when just warm turn out and cool.

sweet pastry 'rags'
cenci

These crisp little pastries are often made at festival times and come in all sorts of shapes and sizes. You can flavour them with grated orange or lemon zest, or orange flower water and they are delicious served with ice cream. They can be made a day or two in advance, as long as they are kept in an airtight container. Alchermes is a pink Italian liqueur, but you could use Marsala or a rich sherry instead, if you prefer.

300 g plain white flour
2 eggs, beaten
2 tablespoons light olive oil
2 tablespoons caster sugar
2 tablespoons Vin Santo or Alchermes
vegetable oil, for deep-frying
icing sugar, to dust

a deep-fryer

serves 12

Sift the flour into a bowl and make a well in the centre. Pour in the eggs, olive oil, sugar and Vin Santo. Mix with a knife to combine, then bring together with your hands and knead into a smooth ball. The dough will be very soft at this point. Wrap in cling film and chill for 1 hour.

Heat the oil in a deep-fryer to 180°C (350°F) – a piece of stale bread dropped in should turn golden in a few seconds. Roll the pastry out very thinly on a floured surface. You may like to do this in two batches. Cut into 3 x 10 cm ribbons with a crinkled pastry wheel. Carefully tie each ribbon into a knot then deep-fry until pale golden brown and crisp. Do not allow to go dark brown or they will taste bitter. Drain on kitchen paper. When cold, dust with icing sugar and serve piled up high on a plate.

ricotta and lemon fritters
frittelle di ricotta

Fluffy little puffs like this are very popular, and are found in all different guises. There is usually one to suit each saint, for his or her particular saint's day. Deep-fried snacks like these are part of Italian life and are seen as a real festive treat. (See picture, page 134.)

250 g ricotta cheese
2 eggs, at room temperature
3 tablespoons sugar or acacia honey
finely grated zest of 1 unwaxed lemon
1 teaspoon real vanilla essence
120 g plain white flour
1 heaped teaspoon baking powder
½ teaspoon sea salt
vegetable oil, for deep-frying
icing sugar, to serve

a deep-fryer

makes about 30

Press the ricotta through a food mill or potato ricer, or sieve into a large bowl. Whisk the eggs, sugar, lemon zest and vanilla essence until pale and light, then fold into the ricotta. Sift the flour with the baking powder and salt, then fold into the ricotta mixture.

Heat the oil in a deep-fryer to 190°C (375°F) – a piece of stale bread dropped in should turn golden in a few seconds. Have a tray lined with kitchen paper at the ready and a slotted spoon or strainer. Drop heaped teaspoons of the mixture in batches of 6 into the hot oil, and fry for about 2–3 minutes until puffed and deep brown all over (you may have to turn them in the oil). Drain and serve immediately, dusted with icing sugar.

Tuscan wines

Some of the world's most prestigious wines come from Tuscany, but Italian wine laws are a nightmare to fathom so I have tried to simplify the classifications as best I can. Tuscan wine production has progressed in leaps and bounds since the cheap and cheerful wines of the 1960s. Great pains are being taken by producers and oenologists to improve the quality of the wines by restricting the growth on the vines (to improve the quality of a smaller yield); refining the mechanical production process; extending maceration; and ageing in smaller barrels (to soften the tannins).

Most Tuscan reds are based on the Sangiovese grape variety and its clones, which change character according to climate and soil. The grapes are very small with tough dark skins full of tannin (for ageing) and volatile aromas which give the wines their bouquet. The Sangiovese grape is often blended with other grapes to balance its severe nature. But modern methods and painstaking research has enabled the very best to be extracted from just pure Sangiovese without adding any other grapes. Tuscany's geography and geology is so varied that, although the wines are made from similar grapes, they take on individual characters of their own. Let's start by winding our way through the minefield of Tuscan Regional Wine Appellations.

DOCG (Denominazione di Origine Controllata & Garantita)

This appellation guarantees both the origin and quality of the wine. The wines must adhere to strict regulations regarding origin; grape varieties and permitted blends; location of the vineyard; low yields and long maturation; and a characteristic taste. The very first appellation was given to the Vernaccia di San Gimignano in 1966. Every appellation has a *consorzio* (consortium) which helps the producers to understand the complicated appellation laws. It also organizes meetings, wine tastings and wine awards to promote the wines. Each *consorzio* represents its producers at Italy's most important annual wine fair, Vinitaly. Luckily there are only six Tuscan DOCG category wines compared to the myriad DOCs: Brunello di Montalcino; Carmignano; Chianti; Chianti Classico; Vernaccia di San Gimignano; and Vino Nobile di Montepulciano.

DOC (Denominazione di Origine Controllata)

This guarantees the grape variety, the origin of the wine and regulated yields and maturation periods. DOC wines are numerous and ever increasing – those worthy of note include Bianco dell'Empolese; Bolgheri; Carmignano and Barco Reale di

Carmignano; Cortona; Elba; Morellino di Scansano; Pomino; Rosso di Montalcino; Rosso di Montepulciano; San Gimignano; and Vin Santo Occhio di Pernice.

Vino da Tavola

This refers to a simple table wine with no guarantee of origin or quality. However, the appellation *Vino da Tavola IGT (Indicazione Geographa Tipica)* indicates that at least 85% of the grapes were grown in that area. IGT is a classification of 'typical regional wine' recognized by the EU. Confusingly, some of the greatest Tuscan wines (Super Tuscans, page 153), have the label *vino da tavola* as they are made outside the strict DOC and DOCG regulations.

Chianti and Chianti Classico

Chianti is probably Italy's most famous red wine. It will ever be remembered for its curvaceous, straw-covered *fiasco*, synonymous with 1960s and '70s trattorias. Straw baskets were originally woven around the hand-blown bottles for stability and to prevent breakages during transportation by horse and cart. The wine was made to be drunk when young, fresh and fruity and wasn't for laying down. Nowadays, Chianti is usually bottled in high-necked Bordeaux-style bottles. The young wines are quaffable, dry and bouncing with fruit, whereas aged Chianti is rich, elegant and seductive. Only certain Chiantis are worth ageing and many are made to be drunk young. Chianti is only produced in Tuscany, in strictly delimited areas in Florence, Siena, Arezzo, Pisa and Pistoia provinces. Within this large area are the 8 sub-zones of Chianti: Chianti Classico (Firenze, Siena); Chianti Rufina (Firenze); Chianti Colli Aretini (Arezzo); Chianti Colli Fiorentini (Firenze); Chianti Colli Senesi (Siena); Chianti Colline Pisane (Pisa); Chianti Montalbano (Pistoia, Prato, Firenze); and Chianti Montespertoli (Firenze).

The Chianti grape blend is based mainly on the native Sangiovese (from the Latin *sanguis jovis*, meaning blood of Jupiter), but can include some Canaiolo and Colorino to temper its severity, and occasionally some white wine grapes, such as Trebbiano and Malvasia (added if the wine is to be drunk young and not to be aged). There are many different varieties of Sangiovese, with names like Sangiovese Grosso, Brunello, Morellino and Prugnolo. It is the base of most red Tuscan DOC and DOCG wines.

In the past, Chianti suffered from mass production with little attention to quality. That all changed with the DOCG regulations of 1984, which stated that DOCG wines had to come from mature vineyards of more than 5 years standing. Only 2% white grapes could be added, and no more than 10% non-traditional grapes, like Cabernet Sauvignon, Merlot or Syrah and the wine had to be aged in oval oak or chestnut barrels. Since then, Tuscan wine-makers

Clockwise from top left: Cantine Contucci in Montepulciano; Maestro Aolmo, Cantine Contucci; wine barrels, Cantine Contucci; Abbadia Ardenga wine cellars; wine barrels, Cantine Contucci.

have woken up to the competition they face from wine producers from all over the world. Finally, thanks to the producer-led controls and research strategy of Chianti 2000, the area is producing stunning wines from almost pure Sangiovese grapes, without the addition of white wine to temper it. The wine is aged in smaller oak barriques, giving it a modern edge.

All Chiantis are DOCG wines, including Chianti Classico and the other sub-zones of Chianti (page 151). Chianti Classico wine typically has a picture of a black cockerel (known as the *gallo nero*) on the neck of the bottle. It meets more stringent requirements, primarily with respect to quality, and aged wine is labelled Chianti Classico Riserva. As a rule, Chianti Classico and Chianti Rufina can be kept and aged. If you ever have the chance, follow the Chianti Classico Trail signposted between Florence and Siena, which takes you through the heart of Chianti country into fascinating cantinas in beautiful towns and villages. The only way to discover the wine you like is by tasting, and you will be more than encouraged to do so.

Chianti is aged for minimum of 5 months. Superiore, which has a higher alcohol percentage, and Riserva are aged for a minimum of 12 months. Chianti Classico is aged for a minimum of 6 months, while Chianti Classico Riserva is aged for a minimum of 18 months. Notable producers of Chianti include Antinori; Avignonesi; Badia a Coltibuono; Brolio; Capezzana; Castello di Ama; Castello di Volpaia; Fattoria Selvapiana; Felsina Berardenga; Frescobaldi; Poliziano; Tenuta Fontodi; Isole e Olena; Monsanto; and Montesodl.

Brunello di Montalcino DOCG (Siena)

Grown and made around the hill town of Montalcino, south of Siena, this is one of the world's most prestigious wines. It is named after a cloned Sangiovese grape, Brunello, meaning little brown one, and is made solely from Brunello grapes. It is a long-lived wine due to an extra-long maceration with stalks and skins, which gives it more tannins and therefore extra body. The very best wine is bottled as Brunello di Montalcino, while the lesser wine made from younger vines may be sold as Rosso di Montalcino DOC, a robust and chunky wine made to be drunk when young. Brunello is aged for approximately 3 years, while Riserva is aged for about 5 years. Notable producers of Brunello di Montalcino include Barbi; Carparzo; Altesino; Col d'Orcia; Villa Banfi; Lisini; Biondi-Santi; Il Poggione; Villa Banfi; Poggio Antico; and Argiano.

Carmignano DOCG (Prato)

This area, to the west of Florence, used to be the playground of the Medici family. Due to the particular type of well-drained rocky limestone soil in the area, this Sangiovese blended with a small amount of Cabernet has its own particular character. Carmignano is aged for a minimum of 10 months, while Riserva is aged for a minimum of 20 months. Notable producers include Tenuta di Capezzana; and Ambra and Artimino.

Vernaccia di San Gimignano DOCG (Siena)

This is probably Tuscany's most famous dry white wine. It is made from local grape varietal Vernaccia, around the stunning hill town of San Gimignano. It was known as Vernage in medieval London, but its ancient, richer style has been replaced in recent times by a lighter fresher wine. Vernaccia di San Giminagno is aged for minimum of 4 months, while Riserva is aged for minimum of 10 months. Notable producers include La Torre; Il Raccianello; Monte Olivieto; Vagnoni; della Quercia; Pietrafitta; and Falchini.

Vino Nobile di Montepulciano DOCG (Siena)

This wine is made in the commune of Montepulciano from a blend of Sangiovese (locally known as Prugnolo because of its plum-like colour), Canaiolo and a very small proportion of Malvasia and Trebbiano. It used to be very similar to Chianti, but gaining DOCG status has greatly improved its quality. The addition of white grapes was reduced, if not eradicated, and the proportion of Prugnolo was increased. Only the very best wines from the area are sold as Vino Nobile, while the lesser, younger wines are sold as Rosso di Montepulciano. Vino Nobile di Montepulciano is aged for minimum of 12 months, while Riserva is aged for a minimum of 20 months and up to 5 years for the best. Notable producers include Avignonesi; Poliziano; Boscarelli; Montenero; and Valdipiatta.

Morellino di Scansano DOC

Produced in Scasano, a little-known wine zone south of Grosseto, this wine has become very popular in the past few years. It is produced entirely from Sangiovese grapes (locally known as Morellino), it is rich, robust, rustic and full of character. It is aged in oak barrels for 1 year, then bottled and aged for at least 3 months. Notable producers include Mantellassi; Banti; and Le Pupille.

Pomino DOC

This creamy, yet dry white wine made from Chardonnay, Pinot Bianco and Trebbiano and is produced within a tiny area in the Chianti Rufina region. Red Pomino is made from Sangiovese and Canaiolo, with the addition of Cabernet and Merlot. Pomino is aged for 1 month in oak barriques, followed by 4 months in steel. It is bottled and sold to be drunk straight away. Notable producers include Frescobaldi; and Petrognano.

The Super Tuscans

In the late 1960s and '70s, some Tuscan wine producers started experimenting with non-indigenous French grape varieties, such as Cabernet Sauvignon, Merlot and Syrah, which seemed to thrive in the Tuscan soil and yielded some amazing results. However, it was impossible to classify these quality new-style wines within the DOC and DOCG appellations and producers were forced to give the wine its own particular name and class it as *vino da tavola*. They were coined the Super Tuscans by English-speaking wine buffs and are usually known by their single names, such as Sassicaia, the original Super Tuscan of 1968 (100% Cabernet). This was followed by Antinori's Tignanello in the 1970s, Tenuta dell Ornellaia's Ornellaia in 1985 (100% Merlot), then in 1990, Antinori's Guado al Tasso. Nowadays, most reputable wine producers make a Super Tuscan, which is considered to be the 'gem' of their production.

A Super Tuscan is the supreme expression of quality and skill of a wine producer and his oenologist. The wine can be made with any variety of grapes, blended or pure. The prices tend to be high, due to strict and time-consuming methods of production, namely harsh pruning to give low yields and long, cool maceration to release the tannins, which gives an intensity of colour and body. The wines are matured in new oak barriques, and age well. Prices can soar to hundreds of Euros for just one bottle, and their commercial value can double or even triple in time.

Bolgheri, with its proximity to the coast south of Livorno, has proven itself as the principle place for high-end Super Tuscan production. Some of the best Super Tuscans include the following (producers are given in brackets): Conti Contini Bonacossi (Capezzana); Fontalloro and Maestro Raro (Fattoria di Felsina); Grifi and Toro Desiderio Merlot (Avignonesi); Ornellaia (Tenuta dell Ornellaia); Salamartano (Fattoria Montellori); Sangioveto (Badia a Coltibuono); Solaia and Tignanello (Antinori); Summus and Excelsus (Castello Banfi); Guado al Tasso (Antinori); Lamaione (Frescobaldi); Ripa delle More (John Matta); Valdicapria (Avignonesi); Mormoreto (Frescobaldi); Ser Gioveto; and Roccato (Rocca delle Macie).

Elba (DOC)

The best wines from Elba tend to be sweet, silky and rich and the varieties of grapes used vary. Red and Rosato wines are 75% Sangiovese (Sangioveto), tempered with up to 25% other local varieties. White wines are made from 80–100% Trebbiano Toscano (Procanico) and up to 20% other local white varieties. Ansonica is made from 85% Ansonica Bianca and up to 15% other local white varieties. Aleatico comprises 100% Aleatico grapes, while Moscato is 100% Moscato Bianco. Vin Santo Secco or Amabile is made from 70% Trebbiano (Procanico) and/or Malvasia Bianca, plus up to 30% other local white varieties. Vin Santo Occhio di Pernice is a red Vin Santo made from 50–70% Sangiovese, 10–50% Malvasia Nera and up to 30% other local red varieties.

Vin Santo

Just how Vin Santo came by its name is shrouded in the mists of time. No one can agree why it is called 'holy wine'. The legends, unsurprisingly, all involve the Church. Some say the name refers to the time of making the wine, which was usually during Holy Week at Easter (when the grapes were dry enough). According to 14th-century sources, it is said to refer to a wine that had been used during Mass and was then given to the sick in the hope that it would possess miraculous healing powers. Another story relates that in 1349 a Greek Patriarch was served a local *vin pretto* (pure wine) during his visit to the Ecumenical Council in Florence. He was heard to say in Greek 'This wine is from Xanthos!', thinking it was very like a wine from his native land, but the Florentines mistook his pronunciation and thought he had said *santo*, and this consequently led to the name Vin Santo. Whichever story you prefer, Vin Santo was almost definitely used in the celebration of Holy Mass in times past, being a much valued and precious libation throughout Tuscany.

This nectar-like wine ranges in taste from bone-dry and pale in colour to rich, dark and sweet, depending on the method of vinification. It is traditionally made in small quantities on farms that grow their own wine grapes – both for their own consumption and to serve to guests as an act of hospitality. A bottle of Vin Santo is a much-valued gift as this wine is a symbol of friendship and hospitality, and is generally opened only on special occasions.

Vin Santo is a unique wine, produced in small quantities compared to other wines, such as Chianti, using ancient traditions. The wines differ enormously in style, taste and colour, depending on where they are made and who makes them. It can be a truly great wine, so beware of cheap or bargain bottles – the very process of making the wine is an expensive one, as the yield from dried grapes is much less than fresh. It is a labour-intensive and time-consuming art, and cutting corners leads to inferior results. Let price be your guide, and don't be tempted by Vin Santo liquoroso, which is a cheaper, fortified wine and a pale imitation of the real thing.

Real Vin Santo is made from hand-picked, local white grape varieties such as Malvasia and Trebbiano Toscano, although one variety is made from red Sangiovese grapes and is called Vin Santo Occhio di Pernice). The grapes are slow-dried then crushed and fermented.

Normally harvested in October, the bunches of grapes are laid on straw-lined racks or hung from rafters to dry and concentrate the sugars in the fruit. The weather conditions have to be just right – warm and dry enough to dry the grapes without rotting. This high sugar content yields a wine that is both alcoholic and sweet. It is a passito wine – a wine made from dried or semi-dried grapes. The grapes are ready to be crushed when they have reached a sugar level of about 32%. This can be any time between November and March, but usually happens at the end of January. The concentrated grape juice is transferred into traditional 50 litre oak or chestnut barrels called *caratelli*. A small amount of *madre* (mother) – the lees from the previous batch – is added, in a process similar to using a sourdough starter in bread-making. This is said to be the secret to a real Vin Santo, giving it its true character. The barrels are sealed with wax and the fermentation begins. The casks are traditionally kept in a *vinsantaia* (attic), next to the roof for 3 years. Here it will ferment quickly in the heat of the summer and lie dormant in the cooler months. It continues like this for a couple of years, and by December of the third year it is ready for racking and bottling. Some keep the wine in the barrels for up to 10 years to concentrate the wine and really develop its unique character.

Vin Santo has been awarded 3 DOCs: Vin Santo del Chianti, Vin Santo del Chianti Classico and Vin Santo di Montepulciano. All these wines must be aged in *caratelli* for at least 3 years – and at least 4 for a Riserva. Avignonesi in Montepulciano, the King of Vin Santos, barrel-ages its Vin Santo for up to 6 years. For every 45 litres of grape juice they put in a cask, only about 15 litres of Vin Santo are produced, which shows just how much is lost through natural evaporation through the wood over the years. Avignonesi's Vin Santo ranks amongst some of the world's greatest sweet wines. Lighter Vin Santos are delicious served chilled as an aperitif, but the rich, nutty complex and highly alcoholic ones (over 15%) are best served after dinner, with crunchy almond *Cantuccini* biscuits. Vin Santo is quite simply the essence of Tuscany.

If you wish to buy a good-quality Vin Santo, look for the DOC mark on the lable. Vin Santo del Chianti DOC, Vin Santo del Chianti Classico DOC and Vin Santo di Montepulciano DOC (Normale, Riserva and Occhio di Pernice) have to be aged for at least 3 years. Any of these wines will not be cheap – if they are, don't buy them, as they will not be the real thing.

Some notable Vin Santo producers include Avignonesi, Isole e Olena, Badia a Coltibuono, Villa di Capezzana, Castello di Volpaia, Frescobaldi, Villa di Vetrice, Felsina Berardenga, Castell'in Villa, Giovanni Cappelli, Antinori, Monte Vertine, Pagliarese, Selvapiana, Castellau, Brolio and Villa di Vetrice. I tasted a particularly good Vin Santo from Abbadia Ardenga at La Cantina Museo di Montalcino run by S. Mario Ciacci.

Main picture: Vin Santo barrels at Cantina Abbadia Ardenga; Inset: Mario Ciacci of Cantina Abbadia Ardenga.

websites and mail order

ITALIAN FOOD

Valvona and Crolla
19 Elm Row,
Edinburgh EH7 4AA
Tel: 0131 556 6066
www.valvonacrolla.com
Italian Specialist Wine Merchant of the Year 2005, which also sells an extensive range of deli products.

Carluccio's
28a Neal Street,
London WC2H 9QT
Tel: 020 7240 1487
www.carluccios.com
Quality Italian produce, such as rice, grains, cured meats, pasta, condiments, seasonal truffles, fruit, vegetables, chocolates and gifts.

Baroni Alimentari
Interno Mercato Centrale
Via Galluzzo
Florence, Italy
www.baronialimentari.it
Offers an unbelievable selection of top-quality cheeses, condiments, oils, aged balsamic vinegars, fresh alpine butter, fresh black and white truffles in season, and truffle products. Will ship orders all over the world.

La Fromagerie
30 Highbury Park,
London N5 2AA
Tel: 020 7359 7440
Perfect cheese.

The Oil Merchant Ltd
47 Ashchurch Grove,
London W12 9BU
Tel: 020 8740 1335
The first port of call for olive oil and dressings, oils, sauces, pasta and vinegars – what a selection! Mail order, retail and wholesale.

The Spice Shop
1 Blenheim Crescent,
London W11 2EE
Tel: 020 7221 4448
www.thespiceshoponline.com
Dried herbs, spices, blends, grains, nuts and fruits.

www.camisa.co.uk
Specialist in Italian foodstuffs, from cheeses to charcuterie and pastas to oils.

www.esperya.com
Genuine, high-quality food products from all regions of Italy, including olive oil, pasta, rice, cured meats, seafood, cheeses and wines.

www.savoria.co.uk
Sells 'i veri sapori d'Italia', the true tastes of Italy. Food created by Italian artisan producers from all regions of Italy, including the islands.

www.chefshop.com
Started by a small group of passionate food-lovers with a mission to change the way people think and feel about the foods they eat by finding the very best-tasting foods from small farmers and artisan producers from around the world.

www.italianfooddirect.com
Italian food and wine, including organic produce. Worldwide delivery.

www.nifeislife.com
An online Italian supermarket providing a wide range of Italian food products, including fresh yeast and real pecorino cheese.

www.olivesdirect.co.uk
A selection of the finest quality fresh olives available in the UK today delivered directly to your door.

www.farmersmarkets.net
The National Association of Farmers Markets, promoting farmers markets across Britain.

HERB PLANTS AND SEEDS

Jekka's Herb Farm
Rose Cottage, Shellard's Lane,
Alverston,
Bristol BS35 3SY
Tel: 01454 418878
www.jekkasherbfarm.com
Suppliers of organic herb plants and seeds.

Laurel Farm Herbs
Main Road, A12 Kelsale,
Saxmundham,
Suffolk IP17 2RG
Tel: 01728 668 223
www.theherbfarm.co.uk
Marvellous selection of live herb plants delivered to your door.

www.seedsofitaly.sagenet.co.uk
Real Italian seeds supplied mail order for growing your own Italian fruit, vegetables and herbs.

USEFUL INFORMATION

www.slowfood.com
An international association that promotes food and wine culture, but also defends food and agricultural biodiversity world-wide.

www.agriturismo.net
Holiday accomodation on farms and vineyards in Tuscany.

www.gamberorosso.it
Fascinating Italian gastronomic website with information on books, food and wine.

www.wine-searcher.com
Search engine for finding local importers of Italian wines in the UK and USA.

www.italianwinereview.com
Interesting and impartial news and information about Italian wines

www.menu2menu.com/italglossary.html
Helpful glossary of Italian menu and cooking terms.

www.mycologue.co.uk
The internet mushroom shop. A unique selection of products that will delight anyone interested in collecting, eating, cultivating or simply appreciating mushrooms.

KITCHEN EQUIPMENT

Bartolini
Via dei Servi, 30/r,
Santissima Annunziata,
Florence, Italy
Italian cookware shop, a temple of gastronomy.

Divertimenti
33–34 Marylebone High Street,
London W1U 4PT
Tel: 020 7935 0689
227–229 Brompton Road
London SW3 2EP
Tel: 020 7581 8065
www.divertimenti.co.uk
Two London shops plus mail order for a wide range of equipment. A knife sharpening and copper retinning service is available.

David Mellor
4 Sloane Square
London SW1W 8EE
Tel: 020 7730 4259
www.davidmellordesign.co.uk
Shop, plus mail order catalogue.

www.thecookskitchen.com
Mail order company with everything you could need for cooking Italian-style – you can browse by country – they even have giant pepper mills!

www.cucinadirect.com
Very good mail order kitchenware shop. Products include Italian food hampers and food gifts.

www.lakelandlimited.com
Huge range of high-quality bakeware and cookery equipment available by mail order, online and from their shops. Some hard-to-find ingredients also available. Phone for a catalogue.

index

acknowledgements

This book was photographed entirely at La Casellaccia in Val d'Orcia, Tuscany, which is available for weekly hire. For further information, please contact giorgiomiani@tin.it

Many of the props featured in the photographs are available from:
Ilaria Miani
Via Monserrato 35
00186 Rome
Italy
Tel: (+ 39) 06 6833160

Grateful thanks are due to all the farmers, shop-keepers, market stall holders and local Tuscans who all cheerfully allowed us to photograph themselves or their animals, crops and produce on their land or premises: the owners of La Casallaccia; Ilaria Miani for her beautiful props; Caffe Fiaschetteria Italiana 'La Botteguccia', Montalcino; Ristorante 'Da Mario', Via Soccini 60, Buonconvento (SI) for interior shots; The artichoke families of Chiusure; Chef Lapo Libertini at Osteria/Enoteca Il Pozzo di Chiusure, Chiusure, Asciano (SI); Biancane ar.l. Servizi al Turismo, Asciano (SI); Chef Averino Masci at Ristorante al Casale, Chianciano Terme; La Bottega del Naturista for its incredible pecorino selection, Corso Rossellino, Pienza (SI); Bar Pasticceria Grand Italia, Chianciano Terme for giving us some wonderful candied fruits and rice paper for the panpepato; Pasticceria Mariuccia, Montalcino (SI); Natalino Pedagna and staff at pescheria Golfo di Gaeta, Chianciano Terme (SI) for allowing us to photograph their catch of the day; Mario Ciacci of Abbadia Ardenga at La Cantina Museo di Montalcino, for a fascinating tour of his museum celebrating Tuscan peasant farming, and wine tasting of vin santo (for more information, see www.abbadiardengapoggio.it); the Redi, Contucci, Gattavecchie and Montepulciano (SI) wine cantinas and l'Abbazia di Monteoliveto Maggiore.

All photography by Peter Cassidy except page 152 photograph by Alan Williams.

Thanks to Gabriella Le Grazie for organizing the locations and making it all possible.